mac&cheese, please!

50 Super Cheesy Recipes

Laura Werlin

PHOTOGRAPHY BY MAREN CARUSO

**Andrews McMeel
Publishing, LLC**

Kansas City • Sydney • London

To Dad, whose bemusement at my profession was par
for the course, but whose love and support of the same was
anything but. I hope the mac & cheese is meeting your
standards in that great sky above.

Andrews McMeel Publishing, LLC,
an Andrews McMeel Universal company,
1130 Walnut Street, Kansas City, Missouri 64106.

www.andrewsmcmeel.com

12 13 14 15 16 SDB 10 9 8 7 6 5 4 3 2 1

ISBN: 978-1-4494-2646-0

Library of Congress Control Number: 2012936731

Design: Julie Barnes
Photography: Maren Caruso
Photo Assistant/digital tech: Shanti Colangelo
Food Stylist: Robyn Valarik
Food Stylist Assistant: Alexa Hyman
Prop Stylist: Ethel Brennan
Photography: Ben Pieper; Food Stylist: Trina Kahl, pages 38 and 90

www.laurawerlin.com

ATTENTION: SCHOOLS AND BUSINESSES
Andrews McMeel books are available at quantity discounts with bulk purchase for educational,
business, or sales promotional use. For information, please e-mail the Andrews McMeel Special Sales
Department: specialsales@amuniversal.com

contents

Introduction vi

Mac & Cheese Fun Facts . . . xi Achieving Mac & Cheese Perfection . . . xii

Say Cheese . . . xvi Pasta Primer . . . xxii Turning Bread into Crumbs . . . xxiii

Milk and Cream: Shades of Difference . . . xxiv Getting Saucy . . . xxv And

Speaking of Gluten-Free . . . . . . xxvi Dishing . . . xxvi The Next Day . . . xxvii

Chapter 1   Classic (and Almost Classic) ● 1

Chapter 2   Mostly Cheese ● 23

Chapter 3   Eat Your Veggies ● 41

Chapter 4   Eat Your Protein ● 61

Chapter 5   Breakfast for Dinner ● 81

Chapter 6   Totally Decadent ● 103

Chapter 7   Lighten Up, Cool Down ● 121

Chapter 8   Party Time ● 135

Acknowledgments   154

Appendix   156

Metric Conversions and Equivalents   157

Index   159

introduction

It all happened in an afternoon. Amidst the multitude of pots and pans I'd used to create my very first mac & cheese, I stood and waited in eager anticipation to taste it. I peered through the glass door of the oven and watched as the youthful pale orange glow of the casserole gradually darkened and bubbled, as if discovering its soul.

I continued to wait until its full transformation from cooking to completion and then carefully pulled the dish from the oven, my oven mitts doubling as burn protectors and nurturers of the molten creation. I set it down and watched as its rapid, bubbling enthusiasm slowed to a gentle murmur. I got eye level with it to study its lunar-like surface and see up close the kaleidoscopic colors of its underbelly, clear as day through the glass pan. It was a test of patience, studying rather than indulging.

Finally, I gently lifted my oversized spoon and cracked through the golden bread crumb crust that crowned the thick cheese foundation. Like a diver reaching toward a treasure, I guided the spoon into the depths of the casserole, extracting the creamy noodles as they oozed cheese from their tiny tunnels and remained prim-looking in their orange-colored shrouds. On the plate, the mixture steamed and whistled as I blew, ever so cautious about its heat and yet irrepressibly anxious to dig in.

Finally, it was time. I lifted the spoon to my mouth, and as I did so took in the heady aroma of melted cheese and hot butter. And then, the reward. The nuttiness of the butter-crisped crumbs and the sweetness of the melted cheese that rode piggyback on the velvety noodles transported me to a world of all that was good—warm, welcoming, enticing, and safe. On that day, I learned the true gift of macaroni and cheese.

I didn't grow up with mac & cheese. My mom didn't make it, and even if she had, I probably wouldn't have eaten it. Or maybe I would have if I could have figured out how to extract the cheese sauce from the noodles. I hated noodles, so even if you called it macaroni and slathered it with cheese, I couldn't warm up to it. I was the kid who ate the meatballs and Parmesan without the spaghetti, the ricotta and mozzarella in the lasagna but not the pasta layers. Give me the cheese, but please hold the noodles!

I don't exactly know when it all changed, but I know that I've done my best to make up for lost time in my adulthood. Take the time I went to Italy for a cooking class. There, pasta-making inevitably played a major role. I left nary a noodle behind. In fact, I ate so much that I considered jogging home—from Italy to California, that is.

So while macaroni and cheese does not evoke a childhood memory for me as it does for most people, perhaps it represents even more. It is, in short, a revelation. That a dish could be so transformative both in its physical components—cheese shifting from solid to molten, bread easing from soft to crunchy, dried noodles submitting to their true nature in the presence of heat—and in the mind of its taster is proof that macaroni and cheese is far more than just something to eat. It is an *experience*.

I've learned that it is also a blank canvas. Cheese and noodles are its foundation, but the unlimited world of ingredients beyond that foundation allows for nearly infinite variations on the main theme. The fifty recipes in this book represent that notion, but I will be the first to tell you that there are innumerable options beyond what's here when it comes to spiffing up the basic mac & cheese template.

Not that it needs spiffing up, mind you. Clearly my own first experience with macaroni and cheese proved that even the basic can be nothing short of transcendent. But so too is the addition of something simple like bacon or a less likely ingredient like hazelnuts, as you'll see in the Smokey Blue with Leeks and Hazelnuts recipe (page 35). For me, different cheese combinations, vegetables, fruits, olives, and even wine and gin(!) served as inspiration for mac & cheese mix-ins, which is why many recipes in this book, while delicious as is, feature a suggested add-in or two. That means that while the recipe may not be written to include a particular ingredient, it may lend itself to the addition of that ingredient nevertheless.

In case you are concerned that there may be *too* many choices, rest assured that what I've tried to do is create mostly simple variations. Macaroni and cheese shouldn't be complicated. It should be fun, and the work you go through to make it should be amply rewarded with the flavor combinations that result.

I've also made things easier by designing some recipes for the stovetop and others for the oven. For the stovetop versions, all that's left to make after boiling the noodles is the sauce. Combine the two and presto, no waiting time. Because stovetop versions usually lack the seductive crunch that oven-cooked versions offer, many of the recipes I've devised include ways to achieve that essential texture (cheese crisps, anyone?).

While ease is the norm in this book, I discovered that mac & cheese can also be mighty sophisticated. This theme underlies the Totally Decadent chapter. Those recipes are just what the chapter title implies, and a few of them are more time-consuming than the others. But the results? Totally decadent becomes totally worth it.

On the other end of the spectrum, I've included a few lower-fat recipes too. These are decidedly not low-fat, just *lower* in fat. I did this not only to provide a reduced-calorie option but also to help ensure a place for mac & cheese in your year-round repertoire. It's not just hearty fare for cold weather. For that reason, these recipes can all be made quickly on the stovetop. No hot ovens here. And the recipes themselves? They're so good that you may find yourself making them regardless of their relatively healthy nature. But even if you're against anything low fat in the dairy world (or anywhere else for that matter), I encourage you to make those recipes. Instead of skim milk, use the reduced-fat or whole milk, and instead of low-fat cheeses use regular ones.

In addition to the recipes, you'll learn about the best cheeses for mac & cheese and the best method for making bread crumbs (and the breads to make them with). You'll learn when to add the cheese to make a smooth sauce, and whether mac & cheese can be made ahead (yes!) and how to do it. I've also created simple recipes for enticing toppings and add-ins like salsa, guacamole, oven-roasted tomatoes, fried shallots, and more. And I couldn't resist providing a recipe for the ultimate use of mac & cheese leftovers: fried mac & cheese.

Finally, I must admit that this is the first book I've ever written in which I've included Velveeta. My raison d'être is to promote primarily American artisan cheeses. So why the inclusion? Simply because I discovered that whenever I had the chance to eat Kevin's Mac & Cheese (page 14), I found it totally compelling. I learned only later that the key ingredient is, yes, Velveeta. Then, as I queried people about their favorite childhood mac & cheese, the preponderance of people answered that it was always one made with Velveeta. They loved how it melted and how it created the proper cheesiness. Indeed it does.

I didn't think I'd ever have an experience quite like my first mac & cheese—making one, figuring there's nothing like the first time. But having created hundreds of mac & cheese dishes since, I now know that because of its inherent versatility, making macaroni and cheese is like doing it for the first time every time.

mac & cheese fun facts

- Pasta and cheese recipes, precursors to today's macaroni and cheese, can be traced back as early as medieval times.

- Thomas Jefferson's cousin Mary Randolph is credited with being the first American to memorialize mac & cheese in a cookbook. The year: 1824. The book: *The Virginia Cookbook*. No macaroni? She recommended soaking crackers in milk until soft to make what she called "mock macaroni."

- Despite rumors to the contrary, Thomas Jefferson was *not* the first person to bring macaroni to the New World, even though he wrote about his passion for pasta fairly extensively. He probably helped popularize it, though, by serving it with cheese at a state dinner in 1802. It may have been macaroni pie rather than mac & cheese as we know it.

- Macaroni pie is a mixture of noodles, milk, eggs, cheese, and spices poured into a pie plate and baked. In the Caribbean, where it is most popular, it is eaten as Sunday supper and at weddings, parties, and picnics.

- Kraft Foods introduced boxed macaroni and cheese in 1937. The rest, as they say, is history.

- Americans love their mac & cheese. In any given three-month period, approximately one-third of the United States population will eat macaroni and cheese at least once. About half of all children in the U.S. will eat mac and cheese during that time period.

- According to the *Guinness Book of World Records*, the largest mac & cheese ever made was prepared on September 23, 2010. Cabot Creamery Cooperative of Vermont teamed up with Louisiana chef and celebrity John Folse to make the Cabot cheddar creation. They gathered in Fulton Square in New Orleans, where they shattered the previous record of 440 pounds. Their creation: 2,489 pounds.

- July 14 is Macaroni and Cheese Day in the United States.

- Crayola created a Macaroni and Cheese color crayon in 1993. It still exists today.

- The most popular cheese used to make macaroni and cheese is cheddar.

achieving mac & cheese perfection

You'd think that a dish with just noodles and cheese would be pretty simple. And while it isn't exactly complicated, it's helpful to know a few things to ensure great results every time. Here are the essentials:

- It's the cheese
- Milk matters
- Pasta (size) matters
- Salted water, yes!
- Follow the bread crumbs
- Butter, salted, please
- Getting saucy
- Plan (and make) ahead
- Wait, wait

cheese, please

Needless to say, the significance of the role of cheese in a mac & cheese cannot be underestimated. Quite simply, the cheese is the key to greatness. Fortunately, almost every cheese lends itself to a great mac & cheese in some way or another. A creamy cheese like Brie becomes pure seduction when it's part of a mac & cheese. (Just remove the rind before using.) A hard cheese like Parmigiano-Reggiano won't melt, but its cheesy crunch on top of a mac & cheese is legendary. A fresh goat cheese is not only creamy, but it also serves as the tangy yin to the casserole's rich yang. And basically anything you would put in a grilled cheese sandwich or use in fondue is an excellent candidate for mac & cheese. The important thing is that if it's a firm cheese, you must take the time to grate it. Slices of cheese just won't do. You'll more likely end up with cheese clumps instead of a smooth sauce.

nonfat, low fat, reduced fat—oh help!

Sometimes options are good, and other times they're simply confusing. When it comes to today's milk choices, it's a bit of both. It's nice to have choices, but how do you decide which to use when it comes to mac & cheese? The bottom line is this: Go for the fullest-fat choices that your waistline (and/or conscience) will allow. Almost all of the recipes in this book call for a combination of milk and cream, but the type of milk you use is up to you. More on this further on page xxiv.

small is good

Just as there are infinite mac & cheese combinations, so too is there a seemingly infinite number of pasta shapes and sizes. But just because there are so many choices doesn't mean they're all good for mac & cheese. Quite the opposite. Large-size pasta is almost always a poor choice for a true mac & cheese. That's because the focus becomes the pasta, not the cheese or the other ingredients that may be in the sauce. Also, you want pasta that will attract all that cheesy goodness, not repel it. Sometimes the larger pasta shapes insist on their independence and keep the cheese sauce at bay. That pretty much defeats the purpose of mac & cheese and instead makes it simply "pasta with cheese."

salt the water, not the pasta

If you've ever made pasta in unsalted water and tasted it side by side with pasta that's been made in salted water, you'll instantly understand the difference. Pasta that's been cooked in unsalted water is utterly tasteless. Salting after the fact just won't do, which is why every recipe in this book asks you to put salt—lots of it—in the pasta water before cooking the pasta.

(bread) variety is the spice of life

Making a good mac & cheese isn't just about what's *in* it—it's also about what's *on* it. That's why the bread crumbs you use are just as important as the casserole they're crowning. Quite frankly, purchased bread crumbs are a bit like sawdust, so I strongly encourage you to make your own. Not only will your homemade ones be superior but you will also use up leftover bread. The main advantage, though, is that you'll be able to achieve a coarse, rustic texture, which is key to a spectacular mac & cheese.

salty versus sweet (butter, that is)

Even though there's plenty of salt in mac & cheese, that doesn't obviate the need for salted butter. Think of it as one of the building blocks in the perfect mac & cheese. 'Nuff said.

stir it up

It's easy to be impatient with mac & cheese. Who doesn't want that cheesy goodness *right now*? But as with all good things, it's about patience. In mac & cheese terms, this means getting the sauce to the right consistency before going on to the next step. That right consistency is pretty much like cake batter. You want it thick but pourable, which you achieve by stirring over a relatively low heat and waiting. It will tell you when it's ready, even if that moment comes well after you are.

make it easy, make it ahead

Although there are a few steps to making mac & cheese, luckily any or all of those steps can often be done ahead for the oven-cooked versions. Unfortunately, there are fewer make-ahead options for the stovetop versions, but even elements of those can be done in advance.

For both versions, the cheese sauce can be made, covered with a layer of plastic wrap set against the surface of the sauce, and refrigerated overnight. Likewise, the cheeses can be grated ahead and stored either in an airtight container or a resealable plastic bag and refrigerated.

For the oven-cooked versions, the whole kit and caboodle can be prepped and assembled ahead. Just cool the casserole before refrigerating and don't top with the bread crumbs or other toppings until you're ready to bake it.

did i say patience?

Waiting to eat anything with melted cheese is an exercise in sheer torture. Who wants to wait to dig into all that gooey goodness? But wait you must for maximum pleasure. Although most of the recipes in this book advise waiting 15 minutes before serving, the truth is that the finished dishes can sit for a whole lot longer and not only retain their heat but also develop flavor as they cool. The additional benefit to this is that it makes mac & cheese the ideal dish for company. No last-minute hustle, and all the enjoyment of good food and friends.

GOOD-TO-KNOW MEASUREMENTS
- 8 ounces dried pasta equals about 2 cups.
- All but the Party Time recipes will serve 6 people, and all but the Mushroom, Bacon, and Eggs recipe (page 90) can be doubled and put in a 9 by 13-inch pan to serve a larger crowd.
- The Party Time recipes will serve 12 to 16 people.

- Serving just one or two people? Cut the recipes calling for an 8-inch square (1½-quart) pan in half and cook them in a 4 by 8-inch loaf pan. It works perfectly. Likewise, you can cut the recipes in half for the stovetop versions.
- Six 8-ounce ramekins is the equivalent of one 8-inch square (1½-quart) baking dish. Likewise, eight 6-ounce ramekins will yield the same amount, with a smaller portion size but more portions. This is a good size for a side dish.
- "Coarsely grated" means shreds of cheese that are about ¼ inch in diameter. This is the same as the large holes of a box grater.
- "Finely grated" means tiny shreds of cheese about the size of a thin piece of string, not pulverized cheese crumbs.
- 3 ounces coarsely grated cheese equals about 3 cups.
- 2 ounces finely grated cheese equals about 2 cups.
- 4 ounces crumbled soft cheese, such as goat or blue cheese, is approximately ¾ cup
- 4 sandwich-size slices of bread equals 2 cups coarse bread crumbs.
- One 1-pound loaf of bread equals 7½ cups coarse bread crumbs.

say cheese

So now that you know the fundamentals, it's time to put them into practice. Because mac & cheese is all about melted goodness, it's essential to use cheeses that submit to their full glory when exposed to heat. In other words, use good melters! But those aren't the only cheeses you can use to make great mac & cheese. Every cheese has its purpose. The following is a list of styles of cheese and how to use them for mac & cheese.

easiest-to-find melting cheeses

Asiago (fresh, not aged; often referred to as "fresco")
Cheddar
Colby
Colby-Jack
Fontina (Danish)
Gouda
Gruyère
Havarti
Monterey Jack
Mozzarella
Muenster
Port-Salut
Provolone (mild or medium, not sharp or extra-sharp)
Swiss (including Jarslberg)
Velveeta (I know, I know—it's not cheese)

best-tasting/harder-to-find melting cheeses

Equally good melters, but fuller in flavor. Although not available every-
where, these cheeses can usually be found at specialty grocery stores
and, in many cases, local supermarkets and club stores. It's worth going
the extra mile to find them.

Appenzeller
Bel Paese
Burrata
Cheshire
Comté
Crescenza
Dubliner
Emmentaler
Flagship

Fontina (Italian)
Gloucester
Gruyère (cave-aged)
Mahón
Manchego (sheep's milk cheese; not aged or "curado")
Midnight Moon (goat gouda)
Ossau-Iraty (sheep's milk cheese)
Parrano
Pecorino (fresh, not aged; often referred to as "fresco")
Petit Basque (sheep's milk cheese)
Pleasant Ridge Reserve
Point Reyes Toma
Raclette
Wensleydale

great and grate

These cheeses lend their signature saltiness when mixed with other cheeses in the mac & cheese–making process and their signature crunch and toasty flavors when mixed with bread crumbs for the topping or just sprinkled on top on their own.

Asiago (aged)
Coach Farm Grating Stick
Dry Jack
Gouda (extra-aged)
Grana Padano
Mimolette (*vieille* or aged)
Parmigiano-Reggiano
Pecorino (aged)
Piave vecchio
Ricotta Salata
SarVecchio

creamy, not stretchy

These will add richness, sumptuousness, and just plain goodness to your mac & cheese, but don't ask them to stretch for you. Cheese calisthenics just aren't their thing.

Blue cheese (all)
Brie
Camembert
Epoisses
Explorateur
Fresh goat cheese (also known as chèvre)
Fromage blanc
Fromager d' Affinois
La Tur
Mascarpone
Mt. Tam
Ricotta
Robiola
Saint-André
Saint Marcellin
Taleggio

don't ask them to melt, but . . .

These cheeses are in the small category of cheeses that don't melt, though they do soften. What they do is add great texture and in the case of the saltier cheeses, flavor too. Sprinkle these on top of a mac & cheese or mix them in.

Feta
Halloumi
Paneer
Queso blanco

pasta primer

For the most part, macaroni and cheese is best made with smaller-size pasta. This allows the cheese sauce to play the starring role. If the pasta is too large, it will dominate. Simple as that. However, there are a few recipes here where I felt the larger-size pasta was a good foil for the particular sauce.

You also don't want to choose thin, long pasta shapes like spaghetti or fettuccine either. That's a different animal altogether, and while yes, you could break spaghetti into small pieces and use it that way, I don't recommend it. Pasta that's *too* delicate will make the cheese sauce seem heavy and clunky.

Judging by what's on the pasta shelf these days, it seems as though mini pasta shapes are a growing segment. It had never occurred to me to use these for anything, but when I experimented with them for mac & cheese, I loved the results.

Although every store seems to carry different shapes of pasta, what follows is a list of the most commonly found ones (and their appropriate substitutes) that are best for mac & cheese.

Cavatelli (or medium shell pasta or penne)

Elbow macaroni, small (or mini farfalle or small shell pasta)

Elbow macaroni, large (for recipes with hearty and/or heavy ingredients; or large shell pasta, penne, or regular farfalle)

Farfalle, mini (also called bow tie, but not farfellini; or use small elbow or small shell pasta)

Farfalle, regular (also called bow tie; or use cavatelli, penne, or large elbow macaroni)

Fusilli (or rotini or strozzapreti)

Gnocchetti (or cavatelli, orecchiette, or medium shell pasta)

Orecchiette (or medium shell pasta, gnocchetti, or cavatelli)

Penne, mini (or pennette, mezze penne, or mini farfalle)

Penne, regular (or cavatelli, large elbow macaroni, or farfalle)

Radiatore (or fusilli or rotini)

Rotelle, mini (or mini farfalle or small shell pasta)

Rotini (or fusilli)

Shell pasta, small (also called conchiglie; or use small elbow macaroni, mini farfalle)

Shell pasta, medium (also called conchiglie; or use orecchiette, large elbow macaroni, or farfalle)

Strozzapreti (or gemelli, penne, or fusilli)

turning bread into crumbs

Although a food processor is the easiest way to make your own bread crumbs, it's not the only way. If you are using a food processor, then simply put four sandwich-size slices of bread, crusts removed (optional), into the work bowl and whirl away. You'll end up with 2 cups crumbs, which is what you'll need for the 1½-quart pan that's specified in almost all of the recipes in this book. (For the Party Time recipes, you will need double that amount.) If you don't have a food processor, then you're best off letting your bread get stale by tearing it into pieces, putting it on a baking sheet, and leaving it out overnight. Once it's dry, you can put it in a resealable plastic bag and run a rolling pin or heavy can over it to crush the bread into crumbs. The more rustic, the better, so don't worry if the crumbs aren't uniform.

If you don't have all night to wait, then put the torn-up pieces of bread in a very low oven for 20 to 30 minutes. You don't want to toast the bread; you just want to dry it out.

Finally, if all else fails, then yes, you can toast the bread. Just do so as lightly as possible—long enough to dry it out but not so long that it darkens too much. Remember, these crumbs are going to get baked on top of the macaroni and cheese, so if you start with bread that's too toasted, it will likely burn once it's cooked again. Let the toasted bread cool and then crush away.

milk and cream: shades of difference

It takes a dairy dictionary to navigate the milk section of the grocery store these days. Milk comes in four different concentrations of milk fat— whole, reduced fat, low fat, and nonfat (also called skim). Cream comes in at least three different forms, not counting half-and-half. How does this pertain to mac & cheese? Two words: the sauce. First, a few definitions:

milk
- Whole milk = 3.25% milk fat
- Reduced fat = 2% milk fat
- Low fat = 1% milk fat
- Nonfat = no milk fat

cream
- Heavy cream = no less than 36% milk fat (the best for mac & cheese)
- Whipping cream = at least 30% milk fat and less than 36%
- Light cream = at least 18% milk fat and less than 30%
- Half-and-half = at least 10.5% milk fat and less than 18%

For the purposes of the recipes in this book (other than those in the Lighten Up, Cool Down chapter), I decided that the best combination of dairy to use is reduced-fat milk and heavy cream. I like how the lighter milk interplays with the cream to create a perfect sauce weight. Whole milk and cream play well together too. The fact is, you can use pretty much any combination of milks that you like, or just one milk. Just be sure that cream of some type plays at least a small role for maximum flavor and texture as well as cooking ease. Cream binds the ingredients together and makes a silkier sauce far more efficiently than milk does on its own. However, using all cream makes a mac & cheese a bit leaden, so I'd avoid that.

the lighter the dairy, the slower the cooking

In the Lighten Up, Cool Down chapter, the predominant milks in the recipes are reduced and low fat, and the cheeses called for are mostly reduced fat. That combination can make for tricky sauce making because low- and reduced-fat cheeses can clump. The way to avoid that is to be sure to cook the sauce over a medium-*low* heat and let it thicken slowly. Once the pasta is added, it should all hold together. If it does not, then add a little flour, 1 teaspoon at a time (you don't want it to taste floury), while stirring continuously. This should help your cheese loosen up and become creamy once again.

getting saucy

While the majority of the recipes in this book call for making a simple white sauce, that is not the only way to make mac & cheese. In fact, many people quibble with the notion, saying that mac & cheese is supposed to be as basic as possible—just the macaroni, cheese, and a little milk to hold it together. In my opinion, that results in toasted cheese noodles that are the flavor and textural equivalent of paper. Therefore, I don't recommend it. However, there are ingredients you can use to bind a mac & cheese without going through the sauce-making rigmarole. The added benefit to this method is that you don't need flour, which should come as good news to the gluten-free crowd. Here's how you do it:

For an 8-inch square (1½-quart) dish: Whisk 2 cups milk, 1 cup heavy cream, and 2 eggs in a large bowl. Add 2 cups grated cheese and 8 ounces cooked pasta. Pour into a buttered pan. Top with 1 cup grated cheese, and you're good to go. Cook as directed for the Classic Mac & Cheese (page 4).

and speaking of gluten-free ...

A few of the recipes in the book happen to be gluten-free. While the one with "gluten-free" in the recipe title is a dead giveaway about its content, the others are ones that simply don't call for flour. These include the Smoky Silky Parsnip, Mushroom, and Espresso Mac & Cheese (page 104), Butternut Squash, Gruyère, and Brown Butter Mac & Cheese (page 113), and the Truffle Mac & Cheese (page 115), You can, of course, adapt almost any of the recipes in the book to be gluten-free by substituting the pasta and bread crumbs with gluten-free products, and using cornstarch, amaranth flour, or gluten-free all-purpose flour in place of the wheat flour.

dishing

One of the great things about mac & cheese is that you can change the vessel in which you cook it to create very different presentations.

Want individual servings? Put the makings for the oven-baked Classic Mac & Cheese (or almost any mac & cheese in this book except where otherwise instructed) into individual ramekins or other small baking dishes and cook according to the directions for the pan variety. The only difference is that you may want to check whether they're done about 5 minutes sooner because their smaller size may make for a quicker cooking time.

For muffin-size mac & cheese, put the makings for the Classic Mac & Cheese (or almost any of the oven-cooked mac & cheese recipes) into four buttered 12-cup muffin pans (or better yet, use nonstick), set them on a rimmed baking sheet, top with the bread crumbs (or specified toppings), and bake for about 15 minutes, or until golden brown and bubbly.

Want crackling, crusty slices instead? Another option is to cook a half recipe in an 8 by 4-inch loaf pan (or a full recipe in two pans). Let it cool, then refrigerate until chilled, at least 2 hours. Cut the loaf into ¾-inch-thick slices. Melt 2 tablespoons butter and 2 tablespoons olive oil in a large skillet over medium-high heat. Once the foam subsides, add enough slices to fit comfortably in the pan without touching. (You may need to do this in batches.) Cook undisturbed for 2 to 3 minutes, or until the undersides are a deep golden brown. Flip the slices and lower the heat to medium. Cook until browned, 2 to 3 minutes. Serve right away. (Note this method works best with the simplest macs & cheese. Too many additional ingredients may cause the slabs to fall apart.)

the next day

Few dishes lend themselves to reheating as well as mac & cheese does, or at least the oven-cooked versions. The stovetop ones can also be reheated, but with slightly less success because the butter or oil in the sauce can separate. You may be able to remedy this, though (see page xxvii).

The important question for many people is, can you microwave? The answer is a qualified "yes." If you do it at a low power level (20 percent) for 1 minute for every cup of mac & cheese, you should be able to avoid making your pasta tough. The cooking time will vary depending on your microwave's power.

Here's how to make your leftovers new again:

To reheat an oven-cooked casserole, preheat the oven to 300°F. Cover with foil and bake for 10 minutes. Remove the foil and continue to bake until the sauce is bubbling and the casserole is heated through. The amount of time it takes to heat through will vary depending on the quantity you're reheating and whether you're starting with a chilled dish or one that's at room temperature. Either way, it shouldn't take more than about 15 minutes or so.

To reheat a stovetop mac & cheese, put it in a saucepan set over medium-low heat. Cover and cook, stirring occasionally and making sure it doesn't start to bubble or boil. Cook until heated through, about 15 minutes (depending on the quantity). If the butter (or oil) separates, make a small slurry by mixing equal parts cornstarch and water. Add the slurry by the teaspoon until the mixture starts to come together again. After that, dig in!

CHAPTER 1

classic
(and almost classic)

Classic Mac & Cheese . . . 3

Classic Mac & Cheese (Stovetop Version) . . . 5

Gluten-Free Classic Mac & Cheese . . . 7

**Wisconsin Cheese, Brats, and Onion
  Mac & Cheese . . . 10**

Kevin's Mac & Cheese (aka Velveeta, Baby!) . . . 14

**Cheddar, Bacon, Roasted Tomato, and
  Tabasco Mac & Cheese . . . 16**

Fried Mac & Cheese Squares . . . 21

classic mac & cheese Serves 6

This is a classic mac & cheese in every way but it includes onion. I like the sweetness the onions add, but if you prefer, simply leave them out. The dish will likely make it into your regular mac & cheese repertoire either way.

- 1 tablespoon plus 1 teaspoon kosher salt
- 8 ounces small elbow macaroni
- 5 tablespoons salted butter, plus more for baking dish
- 2 cups coarse, fresh bread crumbs (preferably homemade)
- 2 ounces Parmigiano-Reggiano or Pecorino Romano cheese, finely grated (about 1 cup)
- ¾ cup finely diced yellow onion (about ½ medium onion)
- 2 tablespoons all-purpose flour
- 2 cups whole or reduced-fat milk
- 1 cup heavy cream
- 6 ounces medium or aged cheddar cheese, preferably orange, coarsely grated (2 cups)
- 6 ounces Gruyère cheese, coarsely grated (2 cups)
- ½ teaspoon mustard powder
- ¼ teaspoon cayenne pepper
- ⅛ teaspoon ground or freshly grated nutmeg

Preheat the oven to 375°F. Butter an 8-inch square (1½-quart) baking dish or pan (or six 8-ounce ramekins). Set aside.

Fill a 4- to 5-quart pot about three-quarters full with water and add 1 tablespoon of the salt. Bring to a boil and add the pasta. Cook, stirring once or twice, until tender but firm, about 4 minutes, and drain. Reserve the pot.

While the pasta is cooking, in a medium skillet, melt 2 tablespoons of the butter in a medium skillet over medium heat. Turn off the heat and add the bread crumbs and Parmigiano-Reggiano. Stir until mixed well. Set aside.

Using the same pot you used to cook the pasta, melt the remaining 3 tablespoons butter over medium heat. Add the onion and cook, stirring occasionally, until soft and translucent, about 5 minutes. Slowly whisk in the flour and stir constantly until the onion is coated with the flour, 30 to 45 seconds. Continue stirring for about 2 minutes more, or until the mixture starts to darken slightly and smell a bit nutty. Slowly whisk in the milk, cream, and the remaining 1 teaspoon salt and cook until the mixture is just beginning to thicken and bubble around the edges, 5 to 7 minutes. It should be similar in texture to cake batter. If it's soupy, continue cooking until it thickens. Add 1½ cups of the cheddar, the Gruyère, mustard powder, cayenne, and nutmeg and stir until the cheeses have melted and the sauce is smooth but not too runny. Again, it should be similar in texture to cake batter. If it's soupy, continue cooking, stirring constantly, until it thickens.

Add the pasta and stir to combine. Pour into the prepared baking dish. Sprinkle with the remaining ½ cup of cheddar and top with the bread crumb mixture. Place the dish on a rimmed baking sheet and bake until bubbling and golden brown, about 30 minutes. Let cool for 15 minutes before serving.

Add-Ins

Bacon: Cook 6 to 8 slices bacon. Crumble and add after the cheeses have been added and the sauce is smooth, **and/or**

Oven-roasted tomatoes (page 16): Add after the cheeses have been added and the sauce is smooth, **and/or**

Arugula: Add 6 cups, a handful at a time, after the cheeses have been added and the sauce is smooth, **and/or**

Roasted red peppers: Add ¾ cup coarsely chopped peppers from a jar along with the pasta.

classic mac & cheese
(stovetop version) Serves 6

stovetop

Because this version of the classic isn't baked, it's a bit creamier than the oven-cooked one on page 3. And unlike its baked counterpart, it doesn't have the same cheesy crust. It's still plenty cheesy and crunchy, though, because of the Parmesan bread crumbs. Plus, it's especially great to make when you can't bear to wait 45 minutes for the oven version to bake and cool.

. . . .

1 tablespoon plus 1 teaspoon kosher salt

8 ounces small elbow macaroni

5 tablespoons salted butter

2 cups coarse, fresh bread crumbs (preferably homemade)

1 ounce Parmigiano-Reggiano or Pecorino Romano cheese, finely grated (about ½ cup)

¾ cup finely diced yellow onion (about ½ medium onion)

¼ cup all-purpose flour

2 cups whole or reduced-fat milk

½ cup heavy cream

6 ounces Gruyère cheese, coarsely grated (2 cups)

6 ounces cheddar cheese, preferably orange, coarsely grated (2 cups)

½ teaspoon mustard powder

¼ teaspoon cayenne pepper

⅛ teaspoon ground or freshly grated nutmeg

Fill a 4- to 5-quart pot about three-quarters full with water and add 1 tablespoon of the salt. Bring to a boil and add the pasta. Cook, stirring once or twice, until tender but firm, 4 to 6 minutes, and drain. Reserve the pot.

Melt 2 tablespoons of the butter in a medium skillet over medium heat. Add the bread crumbs and Parmigiano-Reggiano and cook, stirring constantly, until the crumbs are a deep golden brown, 8 to 10 minutes. Watch carefully because they can burn easily. The crumbs will continue to crisp as they cool. Remove immediately from the heat and set aside. (Note: These can be made up to 3 days ahead and stored at room temperature in an airtight container.)

Using the same pot you used to cook the pasta, melt the remaining 3 tablespoons butter over medium heat. Add the onion and cook, stirring occasionally, until soft and translucent, about 5 minutes. Slowly whisk in the flour and stir constantly until the onion is coated with the flour, 30 to 45 seconds. Continue stirring for 1 to 2 minutes more, until the mixture starts to darken slightly and smell a bit nutty. Slowly whisk in the milk, cream, and the remaining 1 teaspoon salt and cook until the mixture is just beginning to thicken and bubble around the edges, 5 to 7 minutes. It should be thick enough to coat the back of a wooden spoon. Add the Gruyère, cheddar, mustard powder, cayenne, and nutmeg and cook until the cheeses have melted and the sauce is smooth but not too runny. It should be similar in texture to cake batter. If it's soupy, continue cooking until it thickens. Add the pasta and stir to combine.

Ladle the mixture into individual bowls and sprinkle with the toasted bread crumbs. Serve right away.

Add-Ins

Salami: Cut a 4-inch piece of your favorite salami into ½-inch pieces. Add to the cheese sauce along with the pasta, and/or

Hot sauce: Add 2 tablespoons of your favorite hot sauce along with the cheese, and/or

Italian parsley: Add ¾ cup coarsely chopped parsley leaves along with the pasta.

gluten-free classic mac & cheese Serves 6

This recipe really doesn't differ much from the Classic Mac & Cheese on page 3. Naturally, the pasta is gluten-free, and instead of flour, the thickener is cornstarch. There are other thickeners you can use instead, including gluten-free all-purpose flour or amaranth flour. As for pasta choices, there's rice-based pasta, quinoa pasta, and myriad others. For that, you're best off experimenting and finding the one you like the most. I think the quinoa variety works particularly well and acts the most like the flour-based pastas.

- 1 tablespoon plus 1 teaspoon kosher salt
- 8 ounces gluten-free small elbow macaroni
- 4 tablespoons salted butter, plus more for baking dish
- 2 cups gluten-free, coarse, fresh bread crumbs (preferably homemade)
- 1 ounce Parmigiano-Reggiano or Pecorino Romano cheese, finely grated (about ½ cup)
- ¾ cup finely chopped yellow onion (about ½ medium onion)
- ¼ cup cornstarch
- 2 cups whole or reduced-fat milk
- 1 cup heavy cream
- 6 ounces Gruyère cheese, coarsely grated (about 2 cups)
- 6 ounces cheddar cheese, preferably orange, coarsely grated (2 cups)
- ½ teaspoon mustard powder
- ½ teaspoon cayenne pepper

Preheat the oven to 375°F. Butter an 8-inch square (1½-quart) baking dish or pan (or six 8-ounce ramekins). Set aside.

Fill a 4- to 5-quart pot about three-quarters full with water and add 1 tablespoon of the salt. Bring to a boil and add the pasta. Cook, stirring once or twice, until tender but firm, 8 to 10 minutes, and drain. Reserve the pot.

Melt 2 tablespoons of the butter in a medium skillet over medium heat. Add the bread crumbs and Parmigiano-Reggiano and cook, stirring constantly, until the crumbs are a deep golden brown, 8 to 10 minutes. Watch carefully, because they can burn easily. The crumbs will continue to crisp as they cool. Remove immediately from the heat and set aside. (Note: These can be made up to 3 days ahead and stored at room temperature in an airtight container.)

Using the same pot you used to cook the pasta, melt the remaining 2 tablespoons butter over medium heat. Add the onion and cook, stirring occasionally, until soft and translucent, about 5 minutes. Slowly whisk in the cornstarch and stir constantly until a paste forms, 30 to 45 seconds. Continue stirring for 1 to 2 minutes more, until the mixture starts to darken slightly and smell a bit nutty. Slowly whisk in the milk, cream, and the remaining 1 teaspoon salt and cook until the mixture is just beginning to thicken and bubble around the edges, 5 to 7 minutes. It should be thick enough to coat the back of a wooden spoon. Add the Gruyère, 1½ cups cheddar, mustard powder, and cayenne and cook until the cheeses have melted and the sauce is smooth but not too runny. It should be similar in texture to cake batter. If it's soupy, continue cooking until it thickens.

Add the pasta, and stir to combine. Pour into the prepared dish. Sprinkle with the remaining ½ cup cheddar and top with the bread crumb mixture. Place the dish on a rimmed baking sheet and bake until bubbling and golden brown, about 30 minutes. Let cool for 15 minutes before serving.

NOTE: For a stovetop version of this recipe, see page 5. Just remember to substitute cornstarch for the flour and gluten-free pasta and bread crumbs for the wheat pasta and bread.

Add-Ins

Bacon: Cook 6 slices bacon. Crumble and add after the cheeses have been added and the sauce is smooth, and/or

Oven-roasted tomatoes (page 16): Add after the cheeses have been added and the sauce is smooth, and/or

Arugula: Add 6 cups, a handful at a time, after the cheeses have been added and the sauce is smooth, and/or

Roasted red peppers: Add ¾ cup coarsely chopped peppers from a jar along with the pasta.

wisconsin cheese, brats, and onion mac & cheese

Serves 6

Although popular at one time, Limburger cheese is now made by just one producer in the United States, Myron Olson of Chalet Cheese Cooperative. When it's at its peak, it is not a cheese for the faint of heart. But Wisconsinites love it, and they especially love to put it on a sandwich of brown bread, mustard, and raw onion. This mac & cheese is a version of that, except that it also has another Dairy State favorite in it as well—bratwurst. If you can't find Limburger or brick cheese (another Wisconsin original), then use Fontina, Havarti, or your favorite semisoft flavorful cheese.

• •

1 tablespoon plus 1 teaspoon kosher salt, plus more as needed

8 ounces small elbow macaroni

4 slices dark rye bread, crusts removed (or use marble rye or pumpernickel)

5 tablespoons salted butter

1 medium red onion, coarsely chopped (about 1½ cups)

4 fully cooked 3-ounce bratwursts, cut into ¼-inch pieces (or use bockwurst or boudin blanc)

Freshly ground black pepper

2 tablespoons all-purpose flour

2 cups whole or reduced-fat milk

1 cup heavy cream

10 ounces Colby cheese, coarsely grated (about 3 cups)

6 ounces Limburger cheese, cut into ½-inch cubes (or use aged brick, Havarti, or Fontina)

2 tablespoons sweet-hot or spicy brown mustard, plus more for serving

¼ teaspoon cayenne pepper

½ small red onion, sliced paper-thin (optional)

Preheat the oven to 375°F. Butter an 8-inch square (1½-quart) baking dish or pan (or six 8-ounce ramekins). Set aside.

Fill a 4- to 5-quart pot about three-quarters full with water and add 1 tablespoon of the salt. Bring to a boil and add the pasta. Cook, stirring once or twice, until tender but firm, about 4 minutes, and drain. Reserve the pot.

Put the bread slices in a food processor and process until the crumbs are coarse. Set aside. If you don't have a food processor, then toast the bread ever so lightly, just to dry it out. Put the bread in a resealable plastic bag and use a rolling pin or heavy can to crush the bread into crumbs.

In a medium nonstick skillet, heat 2 tablespoons of the butter over medium-high heat. Add the bread crumbs and cook, stirring frequently, until toasted, about 5 minutes. Transfer to a plate. Wipe out the skillet.

Using the same skillet, heat 1 tablespoon of the butter over medium heat. Add the chopped onion and cook, stirring occasionally, until soft and translucent, about 5 minutes. Add the sausage and cook, stirring occasionally, until lightly browned and heated through, 8 to 10 minutes. Add black pepper to taste. Transfer to a paper towel–lined plate to drain. Set aside.

Using the same pot you used to cook the pasta, melt the remaining 2 tablespoons butter over medium heat. Slowly whisk in the flour and stir constantly until a paste forms, 30 to 45 seconds. Continue stirring for 1 to 2 minutes more, until the mixture starts to darken slightly and smell a bit nutty. Slowly whisk in the milk, cream, and the remaining 1 teaspoon salt and cook until the mixture starts to thicken and is just beginning to bubble around the edges, 5 to 7 minutes. It should be thick enough to coat the back of a wooden spoon.

Add 2 cups of the Colby and Limburger and cook until the cheese has melted and the sauce is smooth but not too runny. It should be similar in texture to cake batter. If it's soupy, just continue cooking until it thickens. Add the pasta, onion, sausage mixture, mustard, and cayenne and stir just until incorporated. Pour into the prepared pan. Sprinkle with the remaining 1 cup Colby and top with the bread crumbs.

Place the pan on a rimmed baking sheet and bake for 30 minutes, or until the mixture is brown and bubbly. Let cool for 10 to 15 minutes before serving. When ready to serve, garnish with the sliced onion, if desired. Serve with extra mustard alongside.

kevin's mac & cheese
(aka Velveeta, Baby!) Serves 6

My dear friend Kevin Donahue has brought this version of mac & cheese to our friend Faye's New Year's Eve party for more years than he can count. It's always the crowd favorite, probably because it follows in the spirit of the evening: indulgent. Or maybe it's because there's a touch of wine in the sauce. Either way, it may be old-fashioned (it calls for Velveeta, after all), but it provides plenty of inspiration for the inevitable resolutions that follow the next day. Note that the assembled casserole needs to rest for about an hour (and up to one day) before baking, so plan accordingly.

· ·

1 tablespoon plus 1 teaspoon kosher salt

8 ounces elbow macaroni

½ cup sour cream

4 tablespoons salted butter

2 tablespoons all-purpose flour

2 cups whole or reduced-fat milk

8 ounces Velveeta, cut into 1-inch cubes

¼ cup white wine

¼ teaspoon cayenne pepper

¼ teaspoon mustard powder

⅛ teaspoon ground or freshly grated nutmeg

⅛ teaspoon freshly ground black pepper

Butter an 8-inch square (1½-quart) baking dish or pan (or six 8-ounce ramekins). Set aside.

Fill a 4- to 5-quart pot about three-quarters full with water and add 1 tablespoon of the salt. Bring to a boil and add the pasta. Cook, stirring once or twice, until tender but firm, about 4 minutes, and drain. Place the pasta back in the pot and add the sour cream. Mix until the pasta is well coated. Spoon the pasta into the prepared dish. Rinse and dry the pot, but there is no need to wash it thoroughly.

Using the same pot, melt the butter over medium heat. Slowly whisk in the flour and stir constantly until a paste forms, 30 to 45 seconds. Continue stirring for 1 to 2 minutes more, until the mixture starts to darken slightly and smell a bit nutty. Slowly whisk in the milk and the remaining 1 teaspoon salt and stir until the mixture has thickened and is just beginning to bubble around the edges, 5 to 7 minutes. It should be thick enough to coat the back of a wooden spoon. Add the Velveeta, wine, cayenne, mustard powder, nutmeg, and black pepper and cook until the cheese has melted and the sauce is smooth but not too runny. It should be similar in texture to cake batter. If it's soupy, continue cooking until it thickens.

Pour over the pasta in the baking dish. Let the casserole sit for at least 1 hour before baking to allow the pasta to absorb some of the liquid and to allow the flavors to meld. (Note: You can make this up to this point 1 day ahead and refrigerate it. Bring to room temperature before proceeding.)

While the casserole is resting, preheat the oven to 375°F.

Place the dish on a rimmed baking sheet and bake until bubbling and golden brown, about 30 minutes. Let cool for 15 minutes before serving.

cheddar, bacon, roasted tomato, and tabasco mac & cheese Serves 6

You can surmise from the word Tabasco in the recipe title that this is a spicy one. A good one, too. Bacon, cheddar, hot sauce—how could it be better? Here's how: Poach a few eggs and perch them on top of each helping of the mac & cheese. The creamy yolk drizzles down into the pasta to make a sumptuous, spicy, delectable meal.

. . . .

oven-roasted tomatoes

   1 pint cherry tomatoes

   2 tablespoons olive oil

   ½ teaspoon salt

   Freshly ground black pepper

mac & cheese

   1 tablespoon plus 1 teaspoon kosher salt, plus more as needed

   8 ounces small elbow macaroni or small conchiglie (shell) pasta

   4 tablespoons salted butter

   2 cups coarse, fresh bread crumbs (preferably homemade)

   6 slices bacon

   ¾ cup coarsely chopped red onion (about ½ large onion)

   Salt and freshly ground black pepper

   2 tablespoons all-purpose flour

   3 cups whole or reduced-fat milk

   12 ounces cheddar cheese, coarsely grated (about 4 cups)

2½ teaspoons Tabasco sauce, plus more for serving (or use your favorite hot sauce)

½ teaspoon mustard powder

For the tomatoes: Preheat the oven to 400°F. Put the tomatoes on a rimmed baking sheet. Drizzle with the olive oil, salt, and black pepper to taste. Roast for 15 to 20 minutes, until the tomatoes are slightly shriveled. Remove from the oven and let cool. Reduce the oven temperature to 375°F.

For the mac & cheese: Butter an 8-inch square (1½-quart) baking dish or pan (or eight 6-ounce shallow baking dishes). Set aside.

Fill a 4- to 5-quart pot about three-quarters full with water and add 1 tablespoon of the salt. Bring to a boil and add the pasta. Cook, stirring once or twice, until tender but firm, 4 to 6 minutes, and drain. Reserve the pot.

In a medium skillet, melt 2 tablespoons of the butter over medium-high heat. Stir in the bread crumbs and cook just until coated and slightly toasted, about 5 minutes. Transfer the crumbs to a small bowl. Wipe out the skillet.

Using the same skillet, cook the bacon until brown and crisp. Drain on a paper towel–lined plate, reserving 1 tablespoon of the fat in the skillet. When cool, crumble the bacon into bite-size pieces.

In the same skillet, cook the onion in the bacon fat over medium heat until soft and translucent, about 5 minutes. Add salt and black pepper to taste. Set aside.

Using the same pot you used to cook the pasta, melt the remaining 2 tablespoons butter over medium heat. Slowly whisk in the flour and stir constantly until a paste forms, 30 to 45 seconds. Continue stirring for 1 to 2 minutes more, until the mixture starts to darken slightly and smell a bit nutty. Slowly whisk in the milk and the remaining 1 teaspoon salt and cook until the

mixture starts to thicken and is just beginning to bubble around the edges, 5 to 7 minutes. It should be thick enough to coat the back of a wooden spoon. Add 2½ cups of the cheddar, the Tabasco, and mustard powder and stir until the cheese has melted and the sauce is smooth but not too runny. It should be similar in texture to cake batter. If it's soupy, continue cooking until it thickens. Turn off the heat and add the pasta, bacon, and tomatoes, stirring gently to combine. You want to keep the tomatoes intact as best as possible. Pour into the prepared baking dish. Sprinkle with the remaining 1½ cups cheddar and top with the bread crumbs.

Place the dish on a rimmed baking sheet and bake until bubbling and golden brown, about 30 minutes. Let cool for 15 minutes. Serve with extra hot sauce alongside.

Add-Ins
6 eggs: Only if using ramekins, fill the ramekins to within 1 inch of the rim. After the mac & cheese has baked for 20 minutes, remove them from the oven and break an egg into each of the dishes. Sprinkle with salt and black pepper and cook for 10 minutes more, or until the whites have set, or
6 poached eggs: Top each serving with a poached egg. Sprinkle with salt and black pepper and drizzle with a little hot sauce.

fried mac & cheese squares

oven-cooked

Makes about 10 dozen 1-inch squares

There's only one thing better than mac & cheese: fried mac & cheese. Crunchy on the outside, soft and creamy on the inside, it's a dreamy textural sensation, not to mention a flavor-packed one. Best of all, it's a spectacular use of leftover oven-cooked mac & cheese (stovetop mac & cheese won't work here).

The measurements for fried mac & cheese are entirely dependent on how much you have left over. This recipe is enough for a full 8-inch square pan. That's for those of you who are making mac & cheese for the sole purpose of turning it into its fried counterpart.

· ·

1 (8-inch square) oven-cooked Classic Mac & Cheese or
    Buffalo Chicken and Crispy Skin Mac & Cheese (page 144),
    chilled for 24 to 48 hours

1½ cups all-purpose flour

2 teaspoons kosher salt

1 teaspoon cayenne pepper

2 large eggs, lightly beaten

3 cups coarse, fresh bread crumbs (preferably homemade)

1½ cups canola, vegetable, or peanut oil, plus more as needed

Frank's RedHot Sauce, for serving

Preheat the oven to 300°F. Line a baking sheet with parchment paper, and line another one with paper towels.

Cut the mac & cheese into large pieces, then cut each piece into 1-inch squares.

Place the flour, salt, and cayenne in a shallow bowl, and whisk to combine. Place the eggs in another shallow bowl, and put the bread crumbs into a third bowl.

Dip a mac & cheese square into the flour mixture. Tap off excess flour, then dip into the egg. Roll in the bread crumbs and set on the parchment-lined baking sheet. Repeat with the remaining mac & cheese squares.

Heat the oil in a medium pan over medium-high heat. The oil is hot enough when it looks wavy. Test with one mac & cheese square. It should sizzle and begin to turn brown on the underside in about 30 seconds.

To cook, add as many squares as will comfortably fit in the pan without crowding. Using tongs, turn the squares just as they begin to brown on the undersides. Keep turning so that all sides are browned. Transfer to the paper towel–lined baking sheet as they're done. Serve right away or place the batch in the oven to keep warm. Continue cooking the remaining squares.

Serve with Frank's RedHot Sauce alongside.

CHAPTER 2

mostly cheese

Spanish Mac & Cheese . . . 24

Mac & Cheese Meets Grilled Cheese
  (The Ultimate Comfort Food) . . . 27

French Cheese and Savoy Cabbage Mac & Cheese . . . 30

Sonoma Mac & Cheese . . . 33

Smokey Blue with Leeks and Hazelnuts
  Mac & Cheese . . . 35

Garlicky Italian Mac & Cheese . . . 39

spanish mac & cheese

Serves 6

Like Spain itself, this dish is very vibrant. Smoked paprika, piquillo peppers, and extra-crunchy Marcona almonds conspire to create flamenco in your mouth, and the iconic sheep's milk cheese called manchego brings it all together. If you can't find piquillo peppers, use roasted red peppers instead.

- 1 tablespoon plus 1 teaspoon kosher salt, plus more as needed
- 8 ounces medium shell pasta (or use orecchiette)
- 2 tablespoons olive oil
- 2 cloves garlic, minced
- 2 tablespoons all-purpose flour
- 2½ cups whole or reduced-fat milk
- ½ cup heavy cream
- 12 ounces manchego cheese, coarsely grated (about 4 cups)
- 1 teaspoon hot or sweet ("dulce") smoked paprika (*pimentón*)
- ½ teaspoon cayenne pepper
- ¾ cup green olives, pitted and coarsely chopped
- ½ cup Spanish *piquillo* peppers, coarsely chopped (or use roasted red peppers)
- ½ cup Marcona almonds, coarsely chopped (or use skinned almonds, toasted)
- Freshly ground black pepper

Fill a 4- to 5-quart pot about three-quarters full with water and add 1 tablespoon of the salt. Bring to a boil and add the pasta. Cook, stirring once or twice, until tender but firm, 8 to 10 minutes, and drain.

Using the same pot you used to cook the pasta, heat the oil over medium heat. Add the garlic and cook, stirring frequently, until soft but not brown, about 2 minutes. Cook, stirring constantly. Slowly whisk in the flour and stir constantly until a paste forms, 30 to 45 seconds. Continue stirring for 1 to 2 minutes more, until the mixture starts to darken slightly and the oil's aroma is released. Slowly whisk in the milk, cream, and the remaining 1 teaspoon salt and cook until the mixture starts to thicken and is just beginning to bubble around the edges, 5 to 7 minutes. It should be thick enough to coat the back of a wooden spoon. Add the cheese, paprika, and cayenne and cook until the cheese has melted and the sauce is smooth but not too runny. It should be similar in texture to cake batter. If it's soupy, continue cooking until it thickens. Add the pasta, olives, and peppers and stir to combine.

To serve, ladle the mac & cheese into bowls and scatter the almonds on top. Sprinkle each with a couple of twists of black pepper and serve.

Add-Ins

Spanish chorizo: Slice 6 ounces chorizo ¼ inch thick and add along with the pasta, or

Serrano ham: Cut 2 ounces thinly sliced serrano ham into bite-size pieces and add along with the pasta.

mac & cheese meets grilled cheese

(the ultimate comfort food) Serves 8

Imagine using a gooey, cheesy sandwich to scoop up its fork-friendly kindred spirit, mac & cheese. This recipe represents the best of the two in one bowl. All you need to do is make sure you get your sandwich nicely crisped in order to create the perfect textural contrast with the creamy macaroni. Can you spell comfort?

- -

mac & cheese

    1 tablespoon plus 1 teaspoon kosher salt

    8 ounces small elbow macaroni, about 2 cups

    2 tablespoons butter

    2 tablespoons all-purpose flour

    2½ cups whole milk

    12 ounces cheddar cheese, preferably orange, coarsely grated (about 4 cups)

    6 ounces Fontina cheese (preferably Italian), coarsely grated

    ½ cup mascarpone cheese

sandwiches

    2 tablespoons salted butter, at room temperature

    ½ teaspoon cayenne pepper

    8 sandwich-size slices sourdough bread

    8 ounces orange cheddar cheese, coarsely grated (about 2½ cups)

Preheat the oven to 300°F.

To make the pasta: Fill a 4- to 5-quart pot about three-quarters full with water and add 1 tablespoon of the salt. Bring to a boil and add the pasta. Cook, stirring once or twice, until tender but firm, 4 to 6 minutes, and drain.

Using the same pot you used to cook the pasta, melt the butter over medium heat. Whisk in the flour and stir constantly until a paste forms, 30 to 45 seconds. Continue stirring for 1 to 2 minutes more, until the mixture starts to darken slightly and smell a bit nutty. Slowly whisk in the milk and the remaining 1 teaspoon salt and cook until the mixture starts to thicken and is just beginning to bubble around the edges, 5 to 7 minutes. It should be thick enough to coat the back of a wooden spoon. Add the cheddar, the Fontina, the remaining 1 teaspoon salt, and the cayenne, and cook until the cheese has melted and the sauce is smooth but not too runny. It should be similar in texture to cake batter. If it's soupy, continue cooking until it thickens. Add the pasta and mascarpone, and stir to combine. Cover and keep on the stovetop on the lowest heat setting, stirring once or twice while you prepare the sandwiches.

To make the sandwiches: In a small bowl, mix the butter with the cayenne. Butter one side of each slice of bread with the butter mixture. Turn 4 slices of bread, buttered side down, on your work surface. Distribute the cheddar on the bread and top with the remaining bread slices, buttered side up.

Heat a large nonstick skillet over medium heat for 2 minutes. Put the sandwiches into the pan, cover, and cook for 3 to 4 minutes, until golden brown. Turn the sandwiches, pressing each one firmly with a spatula to flatten slightly. Cover and cook for 2 to 3 minutes more, until the undersides are well browned. Turn the sandwiches once more, press firmly with the spatula again, cook for 1 minute, and remove from the pan.

Turn the heat to medium under the mac & cheese just to warm it through.

To serve, cut each grilled cheese sandwich into 4 triangles. Ladle the mac & cheese into bowls and insert 2 grilled cheese triangles on the edge of each bowl. Serve right away.

Add-Ins

Tomatoes: Top the cheese in each sandwich with a lightly salted center-cut tomato slice before cooking, or

Oven-roasted tomatoes (page 16): Add to the mac & cheese along with the pasta, and/or

Smoked paprika: Replace the cayenne pepper in the sandwich, and/or

Pancetta: Cut a 4-ounce piece of pancetta into 1-inch long and ¼-inch wide "sticks" or batons ¼-inch long, and cook in a skillet until crisp. Drain and add to the mac & cheese along with the pasta.

french cheese and savoy cabbage mac & cheese Serves 6

I love to use savoy cabbage in combination with cheese, especially rich and full-flavored cheeses like the French ones called for here, and any starch, potatoes or pasta. Savoy is not bitter like its cabbage brethren, and it makes for a great textural and flavor contrast to the starch and dairy. Although readily available in most grocery stores these days, if you can't find savoy, regular green cabbage makes a fine substitute.

• •

1 tablespoon plus 1 teaspoon kosher salt, plus more as needed

8 ounces medium shell pasta (or use orecchiette)

6 tablespoons salted butter

1 small baguette (about 12 inches; or use half a full-size baguette), made into bread crumbs (see page xxiii)

1 medium onion (about 8 ounces), coarsely chopped

1 large head savoy cabbage (about 1½ pounds), cored, large stems removed, and coarsely chopped (or use half of a regular green cabbage)

Freshly ground black pepper

2 tablespoons all-purpose flour

1½ cups whole or reduced-fat milk

1 cup crème fraîche

12 ounces Comté cheese, coarsely grated (about 4 cups) (or use Gruyère)

8 ounces double-cream Brie cheese, rind removed and cut into
½-inch chunks (this is easiest to do if the cheese is cold)

4 ounces Roquefort cheese, broken into small chunks (or use other
creamy but flavorful blue cheese)

¼ teaspoon cayenne pepper

⅛ teaspoon ground or freshly grated nutmeg

Preheat the oven to 375°F. Butter an 8-inch square (1½-quart) baking dish or pan (or six 8-ounce ramekins). Set aside.

Fill a 4- to 5-quart pot about three-quarters full with water and add 1 tablespoon of the salt. Bring to a boil and add the pasta. Cook, stirring once or twice, until tender but firm, 6 to 8 minutes, and drain. Reserve the pot.

While the pasta is cooking, in a medium skillet, melt 2 tablespoons of the butter over medium heat. Turn off the heat and add the bread crumbs. Stir until mixed well. Transfer to a small bowl and wipe out the skillet.

Using the same skillet, melt 2 tablespoons of the butter over medium heat. Add the onion and cabbage and cook until the cabbage is tender and wilted, 5 to 7 minutes. Add salt and pepper to taste and set aside.

Using the same pot you used to cook the pasta, melt the remaining 2 tablespoons butter over medium heat. Slowly whisk in the flour and stir constantly until a paste forms, 30 to 45 seconds. Continue stirring for 1 to 2 minutes more, until the mixture starts to darken slightly and smell a bit nutty. Slowly whisk in the milk, crème fraîche, and the remaining 1 teaspoon salt and cook until the mixture starts to thicken and is just beginning to bubble around the edges, 5 to 7 minutes. It should be thick enough to coat the back of a wooden spoon. Stir in 2½ cups of the Comté, Brie, Roquefort, cayenne, and nutmeg and stir until the sauce is smooth but not too runny. It should be similar in texture to cake batter. If it's soupy, continue cooking until it thickens.

Add the pasta and cabbage mixture and stir to combine. Pour into the prepared baking dish. Top with the remaining 1½ cups Comté and sprinkle with the bread crumbs. Place the dish on a rimmed baking sheet and cook until bubbling and golden brown, about 30 minutes. Let cool for 10 to 15 minutes before serving.

Add-Ins

Cooked ham: Cut a 4-ounce piece of cooked ham into 1/4-inch pieces. Add along with the pasta and cabbage.

sonoma mac & cheese Serves 6

oven-cooked

For those who don't know, Sonoma County in northern California is unquestionably one of the most beautiful places on earth. It's home to many of America's best wineries and has other vast agricultural expanses as well. That's why many cheese makers have long called it home. That bounty and beauty inspired this recipe. Naturally, I've listed substitutes for any hard-to-find cheeses so that you can enjoy this whether or not your cheeses are Sonoma-made.

. . . .

1 tablespoon plus 1 teaspoon kosher salt

8 ounces small shell pasta

4 tablespoons salted butter

2 cups toasted or stale sourdough bread crumbs (preferably homemade)

2 ounces dry Monterey Jack cheese, finely grated (about 1 cup; or use Parmesan)

2 tablespoons all-purpose flour

2 cups whole or reduced-fat milk

1 cup heavy cream

12 ounces Point Reyes Toma cheese, coarsely grated (about 4 cups; or use Monterey Jack)

8 ounces Laura Chenel's Chèvre (goat cheese; or use your local fresh goat cheese brand), pinched into 1-inch pieces

¼ teaspoon cayenne pepper

⅛ teaspoon ground or freshly grated nutmeg

1 wheel Cowgirl Creamery Mt. Tam cheese (about 14 ounces), rind removed and cut into 1-inch pieces (this is easiest to do when the cheese is cold; or use another triple-cream cheese such as Marin French Triple Crème Brie, Saint André, or a double-cream Brie)

Preheat the oven to 375°F. Butter an 8-inch square (1½-quart) baking dish or pan (or six 8-ounce ramekins). Set aside.

Fill a 4- to 5-quart pot about three-quarters full with water and add 1 tablespoon of the salt. Bring to a boil and add the pasta. Cook, stirring once or twice, until tender but firm, about 4 minutes, and drain. Reserve the pot.

While the pasta is cooking, in a medium skillet, melt 2 tablespoons of the butter over medium heat. Turn off the heat and add the bread crumbs and dry Jack. Stir to combine, and set aside.

Using the same pot you used to cook the pasta, melt the remaining 2 tablespoons butter over medium heat. Slowly whisk in the flour and stir constantly until a paste forms, 30 to 45 seconds. Continue stirring for 1 to 2 minutes more, until the mixture starts to darken slightly and smell a bit nutty. Slowly whisk in the milk, cream, and the remaining 1 teaspoon salt and cook until the mixture starts to thicken and is just beginning to bubble around the edges, 5 to 7 minutes. It should be thick enough to coat the back of a wooden spoon. Add the Toma, goat cheese, cayenne, and nutmeg and stir until the sauce is smooth but not too runny. It should be similar in texture to cake batter. If it's soupy, continue cooking until it thickens.

Add the pasta, and stir to combine. Pour into the prepared baking dish. Sprinkle with the bread crumb mixture. Place the dish on a rimmed baking sheet and bake for 15 minutes. Remove the casserole from the oven and distribute the Mt. Tam over the top. Return to the oven and cook for 15 minutes longer, or until the Mt. Tam has softened and the crumbs are golden brown. Let cool for 15 minutes before serving.

Add-Ins

Rosemary: Add 1 teaspoon finely chopped fresh rosemary along with the cheeses, and/or

Honey: Add 1 teaspoon along with the cheeses, and/or

Golden raisins: Add ½ cup along with the pasta.

smokey blue with leeks and hazelnuts mac & cheese Serves 6

oven-cooked

I created this recipe to showcase one of my favorite American cheeses, Smokey Blue, made by Rogue Creamery in Oregon. If you're not familiar with it, it's a cheese that's just like it sounds—a smoked blue cheese. Although it's become fairly widely available, don't despair if you can't find it. Instead, just use your favorite blue cheese and substitute smoked mozzarella or smoked scamorza for the regular mozzarella. The hazelnuts, also primarily an Oregon-grown product, are the crowning glory on this unusual but delicious mac & cheese.

- 1 tablespoon plus 1¼ teaspoons kosher salt
- 8 ounces small elbow macaroni
- 5 tablespoons salted butter
- 2 cups coarse, fresh bread crumbs (preferably Italian or sourdough)
- 3 leeks, white part only, sliced crosswise ¼ inch thick
- 2 tablespoons all-purpose flour
- 3 cups whole or reduced-fat milk
- 12 ounces mozzarella cheese, coarsely grated, or chopped if water-packed (about 4 cups; or use smoked mozzarella if using regular blue cheese)
- 8 ounces smoked blue cheese (such as Rogue Creamery's Smokey Blue), crumbled (about 1½ cups; or use regular blue cheese)
- ¼ teaspoon mustard powder
- ¼ teaspoon cayenne pepper
- ¾ cup hazelnuts (preferably skinned), toasted and coarsely chopped

Preheat the oven to 375°F. Butter an 8-inch square (1½-quart) baking dish or pan (or six 8-ounce shallow baking dishes). Set aside.

Fill a 4- to 5-quart pot about three-quarters full with water and add 1 tablespoon of the salt. Bring to a boil and add the pasta. Cook, stirring once or twice, until tender but firm, about 4 minutes, and drain.

While the pasta is cooking, melt 2 tablespoons of the butter in a medium skillet. Turn off the heat and add the bread crumbs, stirring to coat. Set aside.

Using the same pot you used to cook the pasta, melt the remaining 3 tablespoons butter over medium heat. Add the leeks and cook until soft, about 5 minutes. Slowly whisk in the flour and stir constantly until a paste forms, 30 to 45 seconds. Continue stirring for 1 to 2 minutes more, until the mixture starts to darken slightly and smell a bit nutty. Stir in the milk and cook until the mixture starts to thicken and is just beginning to bubble around the edges, 5 to 7 minutes. It should be thick enough to coat the back of a wooden spoon. Stir in the mozzarella, half of the blue cheese, the mustard powder, and cayenne and cook until the cheeses have melted and the sauce is smooth but not too runny. It should be similar in texture to cake batter. If it's soupy, continue cooking until it thickens.

Add the pasta, and stir to combine. Pour into the prepared baking dish. Sprinkle with the remaining blue cheese, followed by the hazelnuts. Top with the bread crumbs. Place the dish on a rimmed baking sheet and bake until bubbling and golden brown, about 30 minutes. Let cool for 15 minutes before serving.

garlicky italian mac & cheese Serves 6

oven-cooked

You might think you're eating fettuccine Alfredo when you taste this, but instead, it's an ultra-cheesy and garlicky celebration of some of Italy's best cheeses. But like fettuccine Alfredo, this one is rich. Unlike fettuccine, the pasta in this dish, cavatelli, is short and a little toothsome, making it a wonderful sponge for all the cheesy goodness. If you can't find it, use small or medium shell pasta instead.

• •

1 tablespoon plus ½ teaspoon kosher salt

8 ounces small cavatelli pasta (or use small or medium shell pasta or penne)

¼ cup olive oil

2 medium cloves garlic, minced

2 cups fresh ciabatta bread crumbs (from either a 4-inch square roll or a 4-inch-wide piece from a loaf; no need to remove the crust)

2 ounces Parmigiano-Reggiano or Pecorino Romano cheese, finely grated (about 1 cup)

¼ cup all-purpose flour

2½ cups whole or reduced-fat milk

½ cup heavy cream

6 ounces mozzarella cheese, coarsely grated (1½ cups)

4 ounces Italian Fontina cheese, coarsely grated (1½ cups)

4 ounces Taleggio cheese, rind removed and cut roughly into ½-inch pieces (or just double the Fontina)

¼ teaspoon cayenne pepper

⅛ teaspoon ground or freshly grated nutmeg

Preheat the oven to 375°F. Oil an 8-inch square (1½-quart) baking dish or pan (or six 8-ounce ramekins). Set aside.

Fill a 4- to 5-quart pot about three-quarters full with water and add 1 tablespoon of the salt. Bring to a boil and add the pasta. Cook, stirring once or twice, until tender but firm, 10 to 12 minutes, and drain. Reserve the pot.

Heat 2 tablespoons of the oil in a large skillet over medium heat. Add the garlic and cook for 2 to 3 minutes, until soft but not brown. Turn off the heat and add the bread crumbs and Parmigiano-Reggiano. Stir to combine, and set aside.

Using the same pot you used to cook the pasta, heat the remaining 2 table-spoons oil over medium heat. Slowly whisk in the flour and stir constantly until a paste forms, 30 to 45 seconds. Continue stirring for 1 to 2 minutes more, until the mixture starts to darken slightly and smell a bit nutty. Slowly whisk in the milk, cream, and the remaining ½ teaspoon salt and cook until the mixture starts to thicken and is just beginning to bubble around the edges, 5 to 7 minutes. It should be thick enough to coat the back of a wooden spoon. Add all of the cheeses, the cayenne, and nutmeg and stir until the sauce is smooth but not too runny. It should be similar in texture to cake batter. If it's soupy, continue cooking until it thickens.

Add the pasta, and stir to combine. Pour into the prepared baking dish and top with the bread crumb mixture. Place the dish on a rimmed baking sheet and bake until bubbling and golden brown, about 30 minutes. Let cool for 15 minutes before serving.

Add-Ins

Prosciutto: Cut 2 ounces paper-thin slices crosswise into ¼-inch-wide strips. Add along with the pasta and/or

Leeks: Coarsely chop the white parts only of 3 leeks. Sauté in 1 tablespoon olive oil until soft, about 5 minutes. Sprinkle with salt. Add along with the pasta, and/or

Sun-dried tomatoes: Boil 2 ounces slivered sun-dried tomatoes (not oil-packed) along with the pasta during the last 4 minutes of cooking. Add along with the pasta.

CHAPTER 3

eat your veggies

Truffle, Cream, and Mushroom Mac & Cheese . . . 42

Zesty Kale Two Ways and Fontina Mac & Cheese . . . 45

Eggplant Parmesan Mac & Cheese . . . 47

Indian-Spiced Roasted Cauliflower and Spinach Mac & Cheese . . . 51

Spring Vegetable and Whole-Grain Mac & Cheese . . . 55

Broccoli, Cheddar, and Crispy Shallot Mac & Cheese . . . 57

truffle, cream, and mushroom mac & cheese Serves 6

Truffles and mushrooms are kindred cousins, and so truffle-flecked cheese paired with mushrooms makes a perfect mac & cheese. But not everyone has access to truffle cheese. If that's the case where you live, then use manchego. Or if you can't find that, use Monterey Jack or even Gruyère. You can also drizzle a few drops of truffle oil on top if you have it. But even if you don't, the two cheeses in this recipe, one of which is an indulgent triple cream, will likely make this one of your favorite mac and cheese dishes, no matter what.

• •

1 tablespoon plus 1 teaspoon kosher salt, plus more as needed

8 ounces cavatelli pasta (or use penne)

5 tablespoons salted butter

1 large clove garlic, minced

1 pound mixed wild mushrooms (or use cremini mushrooms), stemmed and cut into ½-inch pieces

1½ teaspoons finely chopped fresh thyme

Freshly ground black pepper

2 tablespoons all-purpose flour

2 cups whole or reduced-fat milk

½ cup heavy cream

12 ounces black truffle cheese (such as Boschetto al Tartufo, Moliterno al Tartufo, or Sottocenere), coarsely grated (about 4 cups; or use pecorino, manchego, Asiago, or Gruyère)

8 ounces triple-cream cheese (such as Saint André, Explorateur, Brillat-Savarin, or triple-crème Brie), rind removed and cut into ½-inch pieces

¼ teaspoon ground or freshly grated nutmeg

Fill a 4- to 5-quart pot about three-quarters full with water and add 1 tablespoon of the salt. Bring to a boil and add the pasta. Cook, stirring once or twice, until tender but firm, 10 to 12 minutes, and drain. Reserve the pot.

In a medium skillet, melt 3 tablespoons of the butter over medium heat. Add the garlic and mushrooms and cook until soft and creamy in texture, 6 to 8 minutes. Add the thyme and a generous amount of salt and pepper to taste. Keep warm.

Using the same pot you used to cook the pasta, melt the remaining 2 tablespoons butter over medium heat. Slowly whisk in the flour and stir constantly until a paste forms, 30 to 45 seconds. Continue stirring for 1 to 2 minutes more, until the mixture starts to darken slightly and smell a bit nutty. Slowly whisk in the milk, cream, and the remaining 1 teaspoon salt and cook until the mixture starts to thicken and is just beginning to bubble around the edges, 5 to 7 minutes. It should be thick enough to coat the back of a wooden spoon. Add the cheeses and nutmeg and stir until the cheeses have melted and the sauce is smooth. It should be similar in texture to cake batter. If it's soupy, continue cooking until it thickens.

Add the pasta and mushrooms and stir until the mushrooms are warmed through and mixture is combined. Ladle into bowls and sprinkle with more black pepper. Serve right away.

zesty kale two ways and fontina mac & cheese Serves 6

Kale seems to have become the vegetable of the moment, which is good news for kale lovers like me. In this mac & cheese, the hearty vegetable appears two ways: mixed into the casserole and also as a crispy topping. Because of this, it almost seems like it's two different vegetables, which makes this not only delicious but also fun to eat.

• •

1 tablespoon plus 1¼ teaspoons kosher salt

8 ounces cavatelli pasta (or use small shell pasta)

12 ounces curly-leaf kale (about ½ large bunch)

5 tablespoons olive oil

¾ cup coarsely chopped yellow or red onion (about ½ medium onion)

1 medium clove garlic, minced

½ teaspoon red pepper flakes

2 ounces Pecorino Romano cheese, finely grated (about 1 cup; or use Parmesan)

Freshly ground black pepper

2 tablespoons all-purpose flour

2½ cups whole or reduced-fat milk

½ cup heavy cream

12 ounces Fontina cheese, coarsely grated (about 4 cups)

¼ teaspoon cayenne pepper

¼ teaspoon ground or freshly grated nutmeg

Preheat the oven to 375°F. Coat the inside of an 8-inch square (1½-quart) baking dish or pan (or six 8-ounce ramekins) with olive oil. Set aside.

Fill a 4- to 5-quart pot about three-quarters full with water and add 1 tablespoon of the salt. Bring to a boil and add the pasta. Cook, stirring once or twice, until tender but firm, about 8 minutes, and drain. Reserve the pot.

To prepare the kale, remove the stems. Cut 4 whole leaves into quarters and coarsely chop the rest. In a large skillet, heat 2 tablespoons of the oil over medium heat. Add the onion and cook for 5 minutes, or until soft. Add the chopped kale and garlic and cover and cook, stirring occasionally, until the kale is tender, 5 to 7 minutes. Stir in the red pepper flakes and ½ teaspoon of the salt and set aside.

Place the quartered kale leaves in a small bowl. Toss with 1 tablespoon of the olive oil, half the pecorino, and salt and black pepper to taste. Set aside.

Using the same pot you used to cook the pasta, heat the remaining 2 tablespoons oil over medium heat. Slowly whisk in the flour and stir constantly until a paste forms, 30 to 45 seconds. Continue stirring for 1 to 2 minutes, until the mixture starts to darken slightly and smell a bit nutty. Slowly whisk in the milk, cream, and the remaining ¾ teaspoon salt and cook until the mixture starts to thicken and is just beginning to bubble around the edges, 5 to 7 minutes. It should be thick enough to coat the back of a wooden spoon. Add 3 cups of the Fontina, the remaining pecorino, the cayenne, and nutmeg and stir until the sauce is smooth but not too runny. It should be similar in texture to cake batter. If it's soupy, continue cooking until it thickens.

Add the pasta and chopped kale mixture, and stir to combine. Pour into the prepared baking dish. Sprinkle the remaining Fontina on top. Distribute the quartered kale leaves over the top. Place the dish on a rimmed baking sheet and bake until bubbling and golden brown, about 30 minutes. Let cool for 15 minutes before serving.

Add-Ins

Dried currants: Soak ½ cup currants in hot water for 15 minutes. Drain and add to the sauté pan with the kale and garlic.

eggplant parmesan mac & cheese Serves 6

oven-cooked

I absolutely love fried eggplant, so I'll use almost any excuse to make it. My love for the vegetable and its signature showcase, eggplant Parmesan, came together to inform this recipe. Time-consuming? A bit. Worth the effort? You bet. To make things simpler, make the tomato sauce ahead of time. Or even easier, simply buy your favorite kind. Note that this dish requires a large cake pan or other 2-quart dish.

. . . .

chunky tomato sauce

1 tablespoon olive oil

1 small onion (about 6 ounces), coarsely chopped

1 medium carrot, peeled and cut into ¼-inch pieces

1 clove garlic, minced

1 (28-ounce) can whole peeled tomatoes, hand-crushed and all juices reserved

2 tablespoons coarsely chopped fresh basil

Salt and freshly ground black pepper

eggplant

2 large eggs, lightly beaten

¾ teaspoon kosher salt

Freshly ground black pepper

¼ cup all-purpose flour

¼ cup fine bread crumbs

¼ cup finely grated Parmigiano-Reggiano cheese

½ cup vegetable oil

1 small globe eggplant (about 1 pound), peeled and cut into ½-inch-thick slices

mac & cheese

1 tablespoon plus 1 teaspoon kosher salt, plus more as needed

8 ounces medium shell pasta

2 tablespoons olive oil

¼ cup all-purpose flour

2 cups whole or reduced-fat milk

1 cup heavy cream

12 ounces water-packed mozzarella cheese, drained and coarsely chopped (or if using vacuum-packed, then coarsely grated)

2 ounces Pecorino Romano or Parmigiano-Reggiano cheese (about 1 cup)

¼ teaspoon red pepper flakes

For the tomato sauce: Heat the oil in a medium skillet over medium-high heat. Add the onion, carrot, and garlic and cook, stirring frequently, until soft, about 5 minutes. Add the crushed tomatoes and their juices to the pan. Decrease the heat to medium and simmer, stirring occasionally, for about 20 minutes, or until thickened. The liquidy juices should be nearly gone. The mixture will thicken as it cools. Add the basil and salt and pepper to taste. Set aside. (Note: This can be made up to 2 days ahead and refrigerated. Or it can be frozen for up to 1 month.)

For the eggplant: Place the beaten eggs in a shallow bowl. Season with a little salt and pepper.

In another shallow bowl, mix the flour, bread crumbs, Parmesan, salt, and black pepper to taste together. Line a large plate or baking sheet with paper towels.

Heat the oil in a 3-quart skillet over medium-high heat. Dip the eggplant slices into the egg and then into the flour mixture. Place in the oil (you will have to do this in batches) and cook, turning once or twice, until golden brown. Transfer to the paper towel–lined plate to drain.

For the mac & cheese: Preheat the oven to 375°F. Oil a 2 by 9-inch (2-quart) round cake pan or other 2-quart baking dish or pan. Set aside.

Fill a 4- to 5-quart pot about three-quarters full with water and add 1 tablespoon of the salt. Bring to a boil and add the pasta. Cook, stirring once or twice, until tender but firm, 6 to 8 minutes, and drain.

Using the same pot you used to cook the pasta, heat the oil over medium heat. Slowly whisk in the flour for 1 to 2 minutes, until the mixture starts to darken slightly and smell a bit nutty. Slowly whisk in the milk, cream, and the remaining 1 teaspoon salt and cook until the mixture starts to thicken and is just beginning to bubble around the edges, 5 to 7 minutes. It should be thick enough to coat the back of a wooden spoon. Add all but ½ cup of the mozzarella (reserve the rest), ½ cup of the pecorino, and the red pepper flakes. Stir until the cheese has melted and the sauce is smooth but not too runny. It should be similar in texture to cake batter. If it's soupy, continue cooking until it thickens. Add the pasta, and stir to combine.

To assemble, spread 1 cup of the tomato sauce on the bottom of the prepared dish. Lay enough eggplant slices to cover the bottom of the pan in one layer. Pour the pasta mixture over the eggplant. Put the remaining eggplant on the pasta. Spread the remaining tomato sauce over and top with the reserved mozzarella. Sprinkle with the remaining pecorino.

Place the pan on a rimmed baking sheet and bake until bubbling and golden brown, about 30 minutes. Let cool for 15 to 20 minutes before serving.

Add-Ins

Ground lamb or ground beef: In a medium skillet, cook 1 pound ground lamb or ground beef over medium-high heat. Use a wooden spoon to break it into small pieces and cook, stirring frequently, until the meat is no longer pink. Season with salt and black pepper. Add along with the pasta to the cheese sauce. (The addition of lamb makes the dish a bit like the Greek dish moussaka.)

indian-spiced roasted cauliflower and spinach mac & cheese

Serves 6

Because cheese isn't a big part of Indian cuisine, it may seem unusual to find an Indian-spiced dish in a book about macaroni and cheese. But East meets West beautifully here with the garam masala–spiced cauliflower, the two cheeses, and the easy-to-make tomato jam. Luckily the garam masala, a blend of spices, is easily found in grocery stores, and queso blanco or halloumi makes a fine substitute for paneer if necessary. If you don't want to make tomato jam, then use purchased tomato chutney or jam instead. Coarsely chopped and salted ripe tomatoes, drained of excess moisture, will also do.

- -

1 tablespoon plus 1 teaspoon kosher salt, plus more as needed

8 ounces medium shell pasta

4 tablespoons unsalted butter

3 teaspoons garam masala

1 small onion, about 6 ounces, cut lengthwise into ¼-inch-wide slices

2½ cups bite-size cauliflower florets

2 tablespoons all-purpose flour

2 cups whole or reduced-fat milk

1 cup heavy cream

12 ounces Havarti cheese, coarsely grated, about 4 cups

6 ounces paneer, cut into ¼-inch pieces (or use queso blanco or halloumi)

½ teaspoon ground ginger

¼ teaspoon cayenne pepper

1 serrano or green Thai chile, seeded and minced (optional)

6 cups baby spinach leaves (about 5 ounces)

Tomato Jam (recipe follows)

Preheat the oven to 400°F.

Fill a 4- to 5-quart pot about three-quarters full with water and add 1 tablespoon of the salt. Bring to a boil and add the pasta. Cook, stirring once or twice, until tender but firm, 8 to 9 minutes, and drain. Reserve the pot.

In a medium bowl, stir together 2 tablespoons of the butter, 2 teaspoons of the garam masala, and ½ teaspoon of the salt. Add the onion and cauliflower and toss to coat. Transfer the vegetables to a rimmed baking sheet. Roast, stirring occasionally, until the vegetables are tender and lightly browned around the edges, about 20 minutes.

Using the same pot you used to cook the pasta, melt the remaining 2 tablespoons butter over medium heat. Slowly whisk in the flour and stir constantly until a paste forms, 30 to 45 seconds. Continue stirring for 1 to 2 minutes more, until the mixture starts to darken slightly and smells a bit nutty. Slowly whisk in the milk, cream, and the remaining ½ teaspoon salt and cook until the mixture starts to thicken and is just beginning to bubble around the edges, 5 to 7 minutes. It should be thick enough to coat the back of a wooden spoon. Add the Havarti, paneer, the remaining 1 teaspoon garam masala, the ginger, and cayenne. Continue to cook until the cheeses have melted and the sauce is smooth but not too runny. It should be similar in texture to cake batter. If it's soupy, continue cooking until it thickens.

Add the pasta, cauliflower mixture, and chile, if desired, and stir to combine. Add the spinach in large handfuls, stirring until each handful wilts a little before adding more.

To serve, ladle into bowls and top with a generous spoonful or two of the tomato jam.

. . . .

tomato jam   Makes about 1½ cups

1 (28-ounce) can diced tomatoes, drained

1 clove garlic, finely chopped

¼ cup red wine vinegar

2½ tablespoons sugar

Salt to taste

Place all the ingredients in a medium saucepan over medium heat. The mixture should bubble ever so slightly but not boil. Cook for about 45 minutes, or until the jam has thickened and most of the liquid has evaporated. Let cool. (You can make this up to 1 week in advance. Store in the refrigerator.)

Add-Ins

Cashews: Sprinkle coarsely chopped roasted cashews over the tomato jam before serving, or

Fried shallots (page 57): Sprinkle over the tomato jam before serving.

spring vegetable and whole-grain mac & cheese Serves 6

stovetop

This dish is the epitome of spring, with its bounty of vegetables and fresh herbs. The goat cheese contributes to the liveliness of the dish, and the Gruyère ties it all together with its legendary melting qualities and nutty flavor. Make sure that you buy sugar snap peas, not snow peas. Then again, if you accidentally get the snow peas, just use 'em. They'll be good too!

. . . .

1 tablespoon plus 1 teaspoon kosher salt, plus more as needed

8 ounces whole-grain rotini pasta (or use fusilli)

4 tablespoons salted butter

¾ cup coarsely chopped spring onion (about 2 large onions; or use 1 small yellow or white onion)

8 ounces shiitake mushrooms, stems removed and quartered

1 cup fresh or frozen peas (no need to defrost if frozen)

6 medium asparagus spears, cut into ½-inch lengths

4 ounces sugar snap peas, strings removed if necessary, halved crosswise

1½ tablespoons finely chopped fresh tarragon, plus sprigs for garnish

Freshly ground black pepper

2 tablespoons all-purpose flour

2 cups whole or reduced-fat milk

½ cup heavy cream

10 ounces Gruyère cheese, coarsely grated (about 3½ cups)

6 ounces fresh goat cheese, cut or pinched into small pieces

½ teaspoon mustard powder

¼ teaspoon cayenne pepper

⅛ teaspoon ground or freshly grated nutmeg

Fill a 4- to 5-quart pot about three-quarters full with water and add 1 tablespoon of the salt. Bring to a boil and add the pasta. Cook, stirring once or twice, until tender but firm, about 4 minutes, and drain. Reserve the pot.

In a medium skillet, melt 2 tablespoons of the butter over medium heat. Add the onions and cook just until soft, about 5 minutes. Add the remaining vegetables and cook, stirring occasionally, for 8 to 10 minutes, until the vegetables are soft and tender. Add the tarragon and salt and pepper to taste.

Using the same pot you used to cook the pasta, melt the remaining 2 tablespoons butter over medium heat. Slowly whisk in the flour and stir constantly until a paste forms, 30 to 45 seconds. Continue stirring for 1 to 2 minutes more, until the mixture starts to darken slightly and smell a bit nutty. Slowly whisk in the milk, cream, and the remaining 1 teaspoon salt and cook until the mixture starts to thicken and is just beginning to bubble around the edges, 5 to 7 minutes. It should be thick enough to coat the back of a wooden spoon. Add the cheeses, mustard powder, cayenne, and nutmeg. Stir until the cheese has melted and the sauce is smooth but not too runny. It should be similar in texture to cake batter. If it's soupy, continue cooking until it thickens.

Add the pasta and vegetables and stir to combine. Ladle into bowls and sprinkle with a little black pepper. Garnish with the tarragon sprigs and serve.

Add-Ins

Artichoke hearts (quartered): Sauté ½ cup frozen thawed or canned and drained with the other vegetables, and/or

Ham: Cut a 4-ounce piece of smoked ham into ½-inch cubes and add it along with the pasta and vegetables to the cheese sauce.

broccoli, cheddar, and crispy shallot mac & cheese Serves 6

I don't know about you, but whenever I was anywhere near a broccoli-cheddar casserole growing up, it was the fried onions on top that I made the beeline for. That memory came to the fore when I was creating this recipe, figuring that the ridiculously good crunchy topping would be even better on mac & cheese. Even though I've provided a recipe for making your own fried onions (or shallots, in this case), feel free to use the canned kind instead (if you go this route, you will need 2 cups). They not only work great, but they also retain the retro spirit of the dish.

- ¾ cup vegetable or peanut oil, plus more as needed
- 6 shallots, cut crosswise as thin as possible, separated into rings
- 1 tablespoon plus ½ teaspoon kosher salt, plus more as needed
- 8 ounces penne pasta (or use medium shell pasta)
- 4 cups broccoli florets, cut into ¾-inch pieces (or use frozen)
- 4 tablespoons salted butter
- ¾ cup coarsely chopped yellow onion (about ½ medium onion)
- 12 ounces mushrooms, quartered (large mushrooms, cut into 6 pieces)
- Freshly ground black pepper
- 2 tablespoons all-purpose flour
- 2 cups whole or reduced-fat milk
- 1 cup heavy cream
- 12 ounces cheddar cheese, preferably orange, coarsely grated (3½ cups)

½ teaspoon cayenne pepper

½ teaspoon mustard powder

⅛ teaspoon ground or freshly grated nutmeg

Preheat the oven to 375°F.

Line a large plate or baking sheet with paper towels.

Heat the oil in a medium skillet over medium-high heat. Working in batches, add a handful of shallots to the skillet and cook just until browned and crisp, 3 to 4 minutes (they will continue to crisp as they cool). Place on the paper towels to drain. Repeat with the remaining shallots, adding more oil if needed. Season lightly with salt and set aside. (Note: These can be made up to 3 days ahead of time and stored in an airtight container at room temperature.)

Butter an 8-inch square (1½-quart) baking dish or pan (or six 8-ounce ramekins). Set aside.

Fill a 4- to 5-quart pot about three-quarters full with water and add 1 tablespoon of the salt. Bring to a boil and add the pasta. After 8 minutes, add the broccoli. Cook, stirring once or twice, until both the pasta and broccoli are tender but firm, 3 to 4 minutes more. Drain, and reserve the pot.

In a medium skillet, melt 2 tablespoons of the butter over medium heat. Cook the onion, stirring occasionally, until soft, about 5 minutes. Add the mushrooms and cook until soft and creamy in texture, 6 to 8 minutes. Sprinkle with salt and black pepper to taste. Set aside.

Using the same pot you used to cook the pasta, melt the remaining 2 tablespoons butter over medium heat. Slowly whisk in the flour and whisk constantly until a paste forms, 30 to 45 seconds. Continue whisking for 1 to 2 minutes more, until the mixture starts to darken slightly and smell a bit nutty. Slowly whisk in the milk, cream, and the remaining ½ teaspoon salt and cook until the mixture starts to thicken and is just beginning to bubble around the edges, 5 to 7 minutes. It should be thick enough to coat the back of a wooden spoon. Add 2½ cups of the cheddar, the cayenne, mustard powder, and nutmeg and stir until the sauce is smooth but not too runny. It should be similar in texture to cake batter. If it's soupy, continue cooking until it thickens.

Add the pasta-broccoli mixture, and stir to combine. Pour into the prepared baking dish. Distribute the shallots (or canned onions, if using) over the top, and top with the remaining cheddar.

Place the dish on a rimmed baking sheet and bake until bubbling and golden brown, about 30 minutes. Let cool for 15 minutes before serving.

Add-Ins

Chicken: Cut 1 pound boneless, skinless chicken breast into ½-inch pieces. Heat 1 tablespoon olive oil in a medium skillet over medium heat and cook the chicken, stirring occasionally, until no longer pink, 5 to 7 minutes. Season with salt and black pepper. Using a slotted spoon, transfer along with the pasta to the cheese sauce, and/or

Bacon: Cook 8 slices bacon until crisp. Crumble into bite-size pieces and add along with the pasta to the cheese sauce, and/or

Sun-dried tomatoes: Cut 2 ounces sun-dried tomatoes (not oil-packed) into thin strips and add with the broccoli to the pasta water to reconstitute. Add the pasta-broccoli-tomato mixture as directed.

CHAPTER 4

eat your protein

Cheddar, Ham, Apple, and Spiced Pecan
    Mac & Cheese . . . 62

Salami, Fennel, Pepper, and Mozzarella
    Mac & Cheese . . . 65

Spicy Reuben Mac & Cheese . . . 68

Vermont Cheddar Mac & Cheese with Ham and
    Maple-Pickled Onions . . . 70

Sauce-and-Meatballs Mac & Cheese with Burrata . . . 73

Andouille, Colby, and Mustard
    Mac & Cheese . . . 76

Prosciutto and Pine Nut Mac & Cheese . . . 79

cheddar, ham, apple, and spiced pecan mac & cheese

oven-cooked

Serves 6

Cheddar and apples are a classic combination, and so too are ham and cheddar. I decided to put them all together in this mac & cheese and give them a Southern twist by adding pecans. The combination ends up being as homey as any mac & cheese can be.

· ·

spiced pecans

2 teaspoons canola oil

¼ teaspoon kosher salt

¼ teaspoon cayenne pepper

⅛ teaspoon ground cumin

⅛ teaspoon ground coriander

⅛ teaspoon freshly ground black pepper

¾ cup pecan halves

mac & cheese

1 tablespoon plus 1¼ teaspoons kosher salt

8 ounces small shell pasta

6 tablespoons salted butter

2 cups toasted or stale bread crumbs (preferably homemade)

2 large shallots, finely chopped

1 tablespoon apple cider

2 tablespoons all-purpose flour

2 cups whole or reduced-fat milk

1 cup heavy cream

12 ounces sharp cheddar cheese, coarsely grated (4 cups)

1 (4-ounce) piece Virginia ham, cut into ¼-inch pieces

2 medium tart green apples (such as Granny Smith or Pippin), peeled, cored, and cut into ½-inch pieces

1 tablespoon grainy Dijon mustard

Freshly ground black pepper

Preheat the oven to 375°F.

For the pecans: In a small bowl, whisk together the oil, salt, cayenne, cumin, coriander, and black pepper. Add the pecans and stir to coat. (It won't look like much coating, but don't worry. It is enough.) Spread the pecans on a small baking sheet and bake until the nuts start to release a cooked nut aroma and begin to brown, about 8 minutes. Remove from the oven and let cool completely. (Note: The pecans can be made up to 3 days ahead and stored in an airtight container at room temperature, or frozen for up to 1 month.)

For the mac & cheese: Butter an 8-inch square (1½-quart) baking dish or pan (or six 8-ounce ramekins). Set aside.

Fill a 4- to 5-quart pot about three-quarters full with water and add 1 tablespoon of the salt. Bring to a boil and add the pasta. Cook, stirring once or twice, until tender but firm, about 4 minutes, and drain. Reserve the pot.

While the pasta is cooking, in a medium skillet, melt 2 tablespoons of the butter over medium heat. Turn off the heat and add the bread crumbs. Stir until mixed well. Set aside.

Using the same pot you used to cook the pasta, melt 2 tablespoons of the butter over medium-high heat. Add the shallots and cook, stirring constantly, until soft, 2 to 3 minutes. Add the cider and cook until all but a teaspoon or so has evaporated. Turn the heat to medium and add the remaining 2 tablespoons butter. Whisk in the flour and stir constantly until a paste forms, 30 to 45 seconds. Continue stirring for 1 to 2 minutes more, until the mixture starts to darken slightly and smell a bit nutty. Slowly whisk in the milk, cream, and the remaining 1¼ teaspoons salt and cook until the mixture starts to thicken and is just beginning to bubble around the edges, 5 to 7 minutes. It should be thick enough to coat the back of a wooden spoon. Add 2½ cups of the cheddar, and cook until the cheese has melted and the sauce is smooth but not too runny. It should be similar in texture to cake batter. If it's soupy, continue cooking until it thickens.

Add the pasta, ham, apples, mustard, and black pepper. Stir to combine. Pour into the prepared baking dish. Sprinkle with the remaining cheddar and pecans. Top with the bread crumbs. Place the dish on a rimmed baking sheet and cook until bubbling and golden brown, about 30 minutes. Let cool for 10 to 15 minutes before serving.

salami, fennel, pepper, and mozzarella mac & cheese Serves 6

stovetop

This recipe calls for fennel seed and fresh fennel along with the salami. However, if you are able to find fennel salami (called finocchiona), then by all means use it. Just eliminate the fennel seed (not the fresh fennel) in the recipe, and enjoy! Balsamic syrup is often located next to the balsamic vinegar.

· ·

2 ounces Pecorino Romano or your favorite Parmesan cheese, finely grated (about 1 cup)

1 tablespoon plus 1 teaspoon kosher salt

8 ounces mini farfalle pasta (or use small shell pasta)

3 tablespoons olive oil

1 small red bell pepper (about 6 ounces), seeds removed and sliced into strips ¼-wide and 1-inch long

½ medium fennel bulb (about 8 ounces), cored and cut into strips ¼-inch wide and 1-inch long

1 small onion (about 6 ounces), cut into strips ¼-inch wide and 1-inch long

1 (4-ounce) piece salami, cut into ¼-inch cubes

1 medium clove garlic, minced

Freshly ground black pepper

2 tablespoons all-purpose flour

3 cups whole or reduced-fat milk

12 ounces mozzarella cheese, coarsely grated (about 4 cups)

1 teaspoon fennel seed

2 tablespoons balsamic syrup

Preheat the oven to 375°F.

Line a baking sheet with parchment paper or a silicone baking mat. Measure out 2 tablespoons of the pecorino. Make a shallow pile with the cheese on the baking sheet. Smooth into a 2½-inch round. Continue with the remaining pecorino, spacing the piles about 3 inches apart. Place in the oven and cook for 8 to 10 minutes, until deep golden brown. Remove from the oven and let cool for 5 minutes. Use a spatula to loosen the cheese crisps. Set aside to cool completely.

Fill a 4- to 5-quart pot about three-quarters full with water and add 1 tablespoon of the salt. Bring to a boil and add the pasta. Cook, stirring once or twice, for 5 to 6 minutes or until tender but firm, and drain. Reserve the pot.

In a large skillet, heat 1 tablespoon of the olive oil over medium heat. Add the bell pepper and cook for 5 minutes, stirring often. Add the fennel, onion, and salami and cook, stirring often, until the vegetables are soft and just beginning to darken around the edges, about 8 minutes. Add the garlic and cook for 1 minute. Add salt and black pepper to taste. Set aside.

Using the same pot you used to cook the pasta, heat the remaining 2 tablespoons olive oil over medium heat. Slowly whisk in the flour and stir constantly until a paste forms, 30 to 45 seconds. Continue stirring for 1 to 2 minutes more, until the mixture starts to darken slightly and smell a bit nutty. Slowly whisk in the milk and the remaining 1 teaspoon salt and cook until the mixture begins to thicken and bubble around the edges, 5 to 7 minutes. It should be thick enough to coat the back of a wooden spoon. Stir in the mozzarella and cook until the cheese has melted and the sauce is smooth but not too runny. It should be similar in texture to cake batter. If it's soupy, continue cooking until it thickens.

Add the pasta, the vegetable-salami mixture, and the fennel seed and stir to combine. Ladle into individual serving bowls and position a cheese crisp vertically about ½ inch deep into the center of the mixture. Drizzle with the balsamic syrup and serve.

spicy reuben mac & cheese

stovetop

Serves 6

This mac & cheese is unquestionably unusual, but I hope that you'll find it unusually good. The spice in it is the Asian chile-based condiment Sriracha, and it stands in for the Russian dressing typically used on Reuben sandwiches. The fiery "Asian ketchup" has become so popular that most grocery stores now carry it. As for the sauerkraut, it lends essential tartness, while the smoky cheese and pastrami put the rich exclamation point on this East-West version of a decidedly Western classic.

• •

1 tablespoon plus 1 teaspoon kosher salt

8 ounces small shell pasta

2 cups sauerkraut

2 tablespoons salted butter

¾ cup finely diced yellow onion (about ½ medium onion)

2 tablespoons all-purpose flour

2 cups whole or reduced-fat milk

1 cup heavy cream

12 ounces smoked mozzarella cheese, coarsely grated (4 cups)

2 tablespoons Sriracha sauce (or use 2 teaspoons of your favorite hot sauce)

1 teaspoon mustard powder

4 ounces pastrami, coarsely chopped

Fill a 4- to 5-quart pot about three-quarters full with water and add 1 tablespoon of the salt. Bring to a boil and add the pasta. Cook, stirring once or twice, until tender but firm, about 4 minutes, and drain. Reserve the pot.

Place the sauerkraut in a strainer. Let the sauerkraut drain, pressing with a wooden spoon to extract as much moisture as possible. Set aside.

Using the same pot you used to cook the pasta, melt the butter over medium heat. Add the onion and cook, stirring occasionally, until soft and translucent, about 5 minutes. Slowly whisk in the flour and stir constantly until the onion is coated with the flour, 30 to 45 seconds. Continue stirring for 1 to 2 minutes more, until the mixture starts to darken slightly and smell a bit nutty. Slowly whisk in the milk, cream, and the remaining 1 teaspoon salt and cook until the mixture starts to thicken and is just beginning to bubble around the edges, 5 to 7 minutes. It should be thick enough to coat the back of a wooden spoon. Add the cheese, Sriracha, and mustard powder and cook until the cheese is melted and the sauce is smooth but not too runny. It should be similar in texture to cake batter. If it's soupy, continue cooking until it thickens.

Add the pasta, sauerkraut, and pastrami and stir to combine. To serve, ladle into bowls and pass extra Sriracha alongside.

vermont cheddar mac & cheese with ham and maple-pickled onions Serves 6

This recipe brings together some of Vermont's best agricultural products—cheddar cheese, maple syrup, and cider vinegar. The result is a very cheesy yet slightly tart-sweet mixture that's refreshing and comforting all at once. Note that the onions need to be made ahead of time, but you can do that two or three days before you want to use them. They get even better after marinating! Just keep them refrigerated.

- ½ cup cider vinegar
- ¼ cup water
- 3 tablespoons maple syrup
- 1 teaspoon finely chopped fresh thyme
- 1 tablespoon plus ¾ teaspoon kosher salt
- Freshly ground black pepper
- ½ medium red onion (about 4 ounces), thinly sliced, then halved crosswise
- 8 ounces small elbow macaroni
- 4 tablespoons salted butter
- 1½ cups coarse, fresh bread crumbs (preferably homemade)
- 12 ounces cheddar cheese (preferably Vermont white cheddar), coarsely grated (about 4 cups)
- 2 tablespoons all-purpose flour
- 2 cups whole or reduced-fat milk

1 cup heavy cream

½ teaspoon mustard powder

¼ teaspoon cayenne pepper

1 (4-ounce) piece maple-cured ham, cut into ¼-inch pieces

Whisk the vinegar, water, maple syrup, thyme, ¼ teaspoon of the salt and black pepper together in a medium bowl. Add the onion; toss to coat well. Refrigerate for at least 1 hour (or up to 2 days), stirring every so often.

Preheat the oven to 375°F.

Fill a 4- to 5-quart pot about three-quarters full with water and add 1 tablespoon of the salt. Bring to a boil and add the pasta. Cook, stirring once or twice, until tender but firm, 4 to 6 minutes, and drain. Reserve the pot.

Melt 2 tablespoons of the butter in a medium skillet. Turn off the heat and add the bread crumbs, 1½ cups of the cheddar, and a generous amount of black pepper. Stir to combine. Set aside.

Using the same pot you used to cook the pasta, melt the remaining 2 tablespoons butter over medium heat. Slowly whisk in the flour and stir constantly until a paste forms, 30 to 45 seconds. Continue stirring for 1 to 2 minutes more, until the mixture starts to darken slightly and smell a bit nutty. Slowly whisk in the milk, cream, and the remaining ½ teaspoon salt and cook until the mixture is just beginning to thicken and bubble around the edges, 5 to 7 minutes. It should be thick enough to coat the back of a wooden spoon. Stir in the remaining cheddar, mustard powder, and cayenne and cook until the cheese has melted and the sauce is smooth.

Add the pasta and ham and stir to combine. Pour into the prepared pan and top with the bread crumb mixture. Place the pan on a rimmed baking sheet and bake for 30 minutes, or until the mixture is brown and bubbly. Let cool for 15 minutes. To serve, use a slotted spoon to scoop up some onion and place atop each serving. Pass the remaining onion alongside.

sauce-and-meatballs mac & cheese with burrata

Serves 6

My friends Linda and Kelly Hayes are big meatball fans. (Well, let's face it: They're equal-opportunity foodies.) They're also great cooks. One time I was enjoying yet another delicious meal at their house, and Linda suggested I do a riff on spaghetti and meatballs for this book. What a great idea, I thought. This dish is unquestionably hearty, and yes, it takes a bit longer than some other recipes in this book, but I promise you, the results are totally worth it. Oh, and the burrata (cream-filled mozzarella) on top? Amazing. If you can't find it, then do yourself a favor and get the best-quality fresh mozzarella you can find.

. . . .

meatballs

1 large egg, lightly beaten

¼ cup ricotta cheese, drained if watery

8 ounces ground pork

1 ounce aged Asiago cheese, finely grated (about ½ cup; or use Parmigiano-Reggiano or Pecorino Romano)

½ slice fresh white or sourdough bread, torn into very small pieces

½ teaspoon fennel seed

½ teaspoon kosher salt

⅛ teaspoon red pepper flakes

mac & cheese

1 tablespoon plus 1 teaspoon kosher salt

8 ounces large elbow macaroni

2 tablespoons salted butter

¼ cup all-purpose flour

2 cups heavy cream

1 cup whole or reduced-fat milk

6 ounces Taleggio cheese, rind removed and cut into bite-size pieces (or use Fontina, coarsely grated)

6 ounces fresh mozzarella cheese, cut into bite-size pieces (or coarsely grated if using vacuum-packed)

¼ teaspoon cayenne pepper

1 recipe Chunky Tomato Sauce (page 47; or use 2 cups jarred)

1 (8-ounce) ball burrata cheese, cut into bite-size pieces (it may fall apart a bit, but don't worry about it; or use fresh mozzarella)

For the meatballs: Preheat the oven to 425°F. Line a rimmed baking sheet with aluminum foil and coat it with a thin layer of olive oil.

Measure out half the beaten egg and discard it or reserve for another use. In a medium bowl, whisk the ricotta and the remaining egg together until combined.

Put the remaining meatball ingredients in a medium bowl. Mix with your hands or, if you prefer, a wooden spoon. Be careful not to overmix or the meatballs will be tough. Add the egg mixture and stir to combine.

Using about 1 teaspoon of the mixture at a time, form the balls in your hand (you may need to put a little olive oil on your hands to keep the mixture from sticking too much). You want the meatballs to be just ½ inch in diameter. Place them on the prepared baking sheet.

Cook the meatballs in the oven for 10 to 12 minutes, stirring once or twice, until they are well browned but not hard. Remove from the oven and set aside. Turn the oven down to 375°F.

For the mac & cheese: Butter an 8-inch square (1½-quart) baking dish or pan (or six 8-ounce ramekins). Set aside.

Fill a 4- to 5-quart pot about three-quarters full with water and add 1 tablespoon of the salt. Bring to a boil and add the pasta. Cook, stirring once or twice, until tender but firm, 6 to 8 minutes, and drain.

Using the same pot you used to cook the pasta, melt the butter over medium heat. Slowly whisk in the flour and stir constantly until a paste forms, 30 to 45 seconds. Continue stirring for 1 to 2 minutes more, until the mixture starts to darken slightly and smell a bit nutty. Slowly whisk in the cream, milk, and the remaining 1 teaspoon salt and cook until the mixture starts to thicken and is just beginning to bubble around the edges, 5 to 7 minutes. It should be thick enough to coat the back of a wooden spoon. Add the Taleggio, mozzarella, and cayenne. Stir until the cheese has melted and the sauce is smooth but not too runny. It should be similar in texture to cake batter. If it's soupy, continue cooking until it thickens. Add the pasta and meatballs and stir to combine.

To assemble, spread about 1 cup of the tomato sauce in the bottom of the pan. Pour the pasta mixture into the pan. Pour the remaining tomato sauce on top of the pasta and top with the burrata. Place the dish on a rimmed baking sheet and bake until bubbling and golden brown, about 30 minutes. Let cool for 20 minutes before serving.

andouille, colby, and mustard mac & cheese <small>Serves 6</small>

It's pretty hard to not fall in love with this combination of spicy sausages and melted cheese. It is definitely rich, though, so the mustard (in the bread crumbs) saves the day with its zippy flavors. (Note: Sometimes it's easier to find the combo cheese Colby-Jack than it is to find plain Colby. If that's the case where you live, then simply eliminate the Monterey Jack called for in this recipe and substitute the Colby-Jack for both cheeses.)

• •

- 1 tablespoon plus 1 teaspoon kosher salt
- 8 ounces large elbow macaroni
- 2 cups coarse, fresh bread crumbs (preferably homemade)
- 2 tablespoons grainy Dijon mustard
- 2 tablespoons olive oil
- 6 ounces cooked andouille sausages, cut into ¼-inch cubes
- 2 tablespoons salted butter
- ¼ cup all-purpose flour
- 3 cups whole milk
- 6 ounces Colby cheese, coarsely grated (about 2 cups; or use cheddar)
- 6 ounces Monterey Jack cheese, coarsely grated (about 2 cups)
- ¼ teaspoon cayenne pepper
- 15 sweet baby pickles, coarsely chopped (about 2/3 cup), plus more for serving
- 1 bunch scallions (8 to 10), white and light green parts, finely chopped

Fill a 4- to 5-quart pot about three-quarters full with water and add 1 tablespoon of the salt. Bring to a boil and add the pasta. Cook, stirring once or twice, until tender but firm, 6 to 8 minutes, and drain. Reserve the pot.

In a small bowl, toss the bread crumbs, mustard, and oil. Heat a medium skillet over medium heat and add the bread crumb mixture. Cook, stirring constantly, until the crumbs turn a shade darker and smell nutty, about 8 minutes. They will continue to crisp as they cool. Transfer the crumbs to a plate and set aside.

Using the same skillet, heat the sausages over medium-high heat, stirring occasionally, until brown around the edges, about 6 minutes. Transfer to a plate and set aside.

Using the same pot you used to cook the pasta, melt the butter over medium heat. Slowly whisk in the flour and stir constantly until a paste forms, 30 to 45 seconds. Continue stirring for 1 to 2 minutes more, until the mixture starts to darken slightly and smell a little nutty. Slowly whisk in the milk and the remaining 1 teaspoon salt and cook until the mixture starts to thicken and is just beginning to bubble around the edges, 5 to 7 minutes. It should be thick enough to coat the back of a wooden spoon. Add the cheeses and cayenne and cook until the cheese has melted and the sauce is smooth but not too runny. It should be similar in texture to cake batter. If it's soupy, continue cooking until it thickens.

Add the pasta, sausage, and pickles and stir to combine. Ladle into individual bowls, sprinkle with the bread crumbs and scallions, and serve with extra pickles alongside.

prosciutto and pine nut mac & cheese Serves 6

I could eat pine nuts every day. I love their richness, their small size, and their crunch. For all those reasons, I thought they'd make a great topping for this mac & cheese. The nuts, along with the prosciutto, which becomes crispy when cooked, make for a double crunch on top of the silky, flavorful filling beneath it.

- -

1 tablespoon plus 1 teaspoon kosher salt

8 ounces medium shell pasta (or use orecchiette)

½ cup sun-dried tomatoes (not oil-packed), slivered

¾ cup pine nuts

4 tablespoons salted butter

2 cups toasted or stale bread crumbs (preferably homemade)

2 ounces Parmigiano-Reggiano or Pecorino Romano cheese, finely grated (about 1 cup)

2 tablespoons all-purpose flour

2 cups whole or reduced-fat milk

1 cup heavy cream

8 ounces Havarti cheese, coarsely grated (2½ cups)

6 ounces Taleggio cheese, cut into bite-size chunks (2 cups; or use Italian Fontina)

2 teaspoons finely chopped fresh rosemary

½ teaspoon mustard powder

¼ teaspoon cayenne pepper

⅛ teaspoon ground or freshly grated nutmeg

2 ounces paper-thin slices prosciutto, cut into ¼ by 1-inch strips

Preheat the oven to 375°F. Butter an 8-inch square (1½-quart) baking dish or pan (or six 8-ounce ramekins). Set aside.

Fill a 4- to 5-quart pot about three-quarters full with water and add 1 tablespoon of the salt. Bring to a boil and add the pasta and sun-dried tomatoes. Cook, stirring once or twice, until tender but firm, 8 to 10 minutes, and drain. Reserve the pot.

Heat a medium skillet over medium-low heat. Add the pine nuts and cook, shaking the pan constantly, until they are a light golden color. Watch carefully, because they burn easily. Remove from the heat and transfer to a small bowl.

Using the same skillet, melt 2 tablespoons of the butter over medium heat. Turn off the heat and add the bread crumbs, Parmigiano-Reggiano, and pine nuts. Stir until mixed well. Set aside.

Using the same pot you used to cook the pasta, melt the remaining 2 tablespoons butter over medium heat. Slowly whisk in the flour and stir constantly until a paste forms, 30 to 45 seconds. Continue stirring for 1 to 2 minutes more, until the mixture starts to darken slightly and smell a bit nutty. Slowly whisk in the milk, cream, and the remaining 1 teaspoon salt and cook until the mixture starts to thicken and is just beginning to bubble around the edges, 5 to 7 minutes. It should be thick enough to coat the back of a wooden spoon. Add the Havarti, Taleggio, rosemary, mustard powder, cayenne, and nutmeg and stir until the sauce is smooth but not too runny. It should be similar in texture to cake batter. If it's soupy, continue cooking until it thickens.

Add the pasta and stir to combine. Pour into the prepared baking dish. Top with the bread crumb mixture and scatter the prosciutto strips over the bread crumbs. Place the dish on a rimmed baking sheet and bake until the prosciutto is crisp and the mac & cheese is bubbling and golden brown, about 30 minutes. Let cool for 10 to 15 minutes before serving.

CHAPTER 5

breakfast for dinner

Gruyère, Caramelized Onion, Blue Cheese, and Bacon Mac & Cheese . . . 82

"Eggs Benedict" Mac & Cheese . . . 85

Waffle Mac & Cheese . . . 88

Mushroom, Bacon, and Eggs Mac & Cheese . . . 90

Spicy "Home Fries" Mac & Cheese . . . 93

Huevos Rancheros Mac & Cheese . . . 96

Fruit and (Mac &) Cheese . . . 100

gruyère, caramelized onion, blue cheese, and bacon mac & cheese Serves 6

When a staffer at the University of California, San Francisco, tasted this, her immediate comment was "Quiche!" Although I hadn't thought of that, I think she was on to something. The bacon-onion-cheese trio is indeed reminiscent of the brunch dish. But because it's not quiche, and because it has a little blue cheese in it, this dish is unique unto itself. Call it what you will, but all you really need to know is that gooey Gruyère, sweet onion, salty bacon, and blue cheese together make one heck of a mac & cheese any time of the day.

• •

1 tablespoon plus 1 teaspoon kosher salt, plus more as needed

8 ounces small shell pasta

8 slices bacon

1 medium onion (about 8 ounces), thinly sliced

Freshly ground black pepper

2 cups coarse, fresh bread crumbs (preferably homemade)

1 teaspoon finely chopped fresh thyme

2 tablespoons salted butter

2 tablespoons all-purpose flour

2 cups whole or reduced-fat milk

1 cup heavy cream

12 ounces Gruyère cheese, coarsely grated (about 4 cups)

4 ounces blue cheese (such as Pt. Reyes Original Blue, Maytag, Roquefort, or Stilton)

½ teaspoon mustard powder

¼ teaspoon ground or freshly grated nutmeg

Preheat the oven to 375°F. Butter an 8-inch square (1½-quart) baking dish or pan (or six 8-ounce ramekins). Set aside.

Fill a 4- to 5-quart pot about three-quarters full with water and add 1 tablespoon of the salt. Bring to a boil and add the pasta. Cook, stirring once or twice, until tender but firm, 4 to 6 minutes, and drain. Reserve the pot.

In a large skillet, cook the bacon until crisp. Transfer to a paper towel–lined plate. Pour all but about 2 tablespoons of the bacon fat into a heatproof jar and reserve. Crumble the bacon into bite-size pieces when cool.

Using the same skillet, reheat the 2 tablespoons bacon fat over low heat. Add the onion and cook, stirring occasionally, until golden, 20 to 30 minutes. If the onion is dry, add a little water, 1 tablespoon at a time. Add salt and pepper to taste.

Put the bread crumbs and thyme in a small bowl and drizzle with 2 tablespoons of the reserved bacon fat. Stir until well mixed. Set aside.

Using the same pot you used to cook the pasta, melt the butter over medium heat. Slowly whisk in the flour and stir constantly until a paste forms, 30 to 45 seconds. Continue stirring for 1 to 2 minutes, until the mixture starts to darken slightly and smell a bit nutty. Slowly whisk in the milk, cream, and the remaining 1 teaspoon salt and cook until the mixture starts to thicken and is just beginning to bubble around the edges, 5 to 7 minutes. It should be thick enough to coat the back of a wooden spoon Add 2½ cups of the Gruyère, the blue cheese, mustard powder, and nutmeg. Stir until the cheese has melted and the sauce is smooth but not too runny. It should be similar in texture to cake batter. If it's soupy, continue cooking until it thickens.

Add the pasta, half the onion, and half the bacon and stir to combine. Pour into the prepared baking dish. Distribute the remaining Gruyère over the top, followed by the remaining onion. Follow with the bread crumb mixture, and top with the remaining bacon. Place the dish on a rimmed baking sheet and bake until bubbling and golden brown, about 30 minutes. Let cool for 15 minutes before serving.

Add-Ins

Ground beef: In a medium skillet over medium heat, sauté 4 ounces ground beef, breaking it into small pieces with a wooden spoon. Season well with salt and black pepper. Use a slotted spoon to add the meat along with the pasta.

"eggs benedict" mac & cheese Serves 6

oven-cooked

Even though eggs Benedict has hollandaise sauce and this mac & cheese version does not have that, my version of the classic brunch dish lacks no richness. Note that this recipe calls for 8-ounce ramekins rather than a single baking dish. That's because the eggs nestle a bit more cooperatively on the bacon and English muffin when they're resting in a ramekin. However, with a couple of adjustments, it can work in a baking dish as well. See the note at the end of the recipe for directions.

• •

1 tablespoon plus 1 teaspoon kosher salt, plus more as needed

8 ounces mini farfalle pasta (or use small elbow macaroni)

3 English muffins, split in half

5 tablespoons salted butter, at room temperature

2 tablespoons all-purpose flour

1½ cups whole or reduced-fat milk

1½ cups plus 3 tablespoons heavy cream

12 ounces Fontina cheese, coarsely grated (4 cups)

½ teaspoon mustard powder

¼ teaspoon cayenne pepper

1 (10-ounce) package frozen chopped spinach, thawed, water squeezed out

6 slices Canadian bacon

6 large eggs, at room temperature

Freshly ground black pepper

1 tablespoon fresh lemon juice

Preheat the oven to 375°F. Butter six 8-ounce ramekins. Set aside.

Fill a 4- to 5-quart pot about three-quarters full with water and add 1 tablespoon of the salt. Bring to a boil and add the pasta. Cook, stirring once or twice, until tender but firm, about 4 minutes, and drain. Reserve the pot.

Place the English muffins cut side up on a rimmed baking sheet and spread them with 2 tablespoons of the butter. Toast in the oven until light brown around the edges, about 10 minutes. Remove from the oven and transfer the muffins to a plate. Reserve the baking sheet.

Using the same pot you used to cook the pasta, melt the remaining 3 tablespoons butter over medium heat until browned. Watch carefully and be careful not to burn it. Slowly whisk in the flour and stir constantly until a paste forms, 30 to 45 seconds. Continue stirring for about 2 minutes more, or until the mixture starts to darken slightly and smell a bit nutty. Slowly whisk in the milk, 1½ cups of the cream, and the remaining 1 teaspoon salt and cook until the mixture starts to thicken and is just beginning to bubble around the edges, 5 to 7 minutes. It should be thick enough to coat the back of a wooden spoon. Add the cheese, mustard powder, and cayenne and stir until the cheese is melted and the sauce is smooth and not too runny. It should be similar in texture to cake batter. If it's soupy, continue cooking until it thickens.

Add the pasta and spinach and stir to combine. Fill the ramekins with the mixture to within 1 inch of the rim. Place on the reserved baking sheet and bake for 15 minutes.

Remove from the oven and top each with an English muffin, cut side up, followed by a slice of bacon. Break 1 egg into a small bowl or shallow baking dish. Carefully pour the egg on top of the bacon. Repeat with the remaining eggs. Drizzle each ramekin with the remaining cream and sprinkle with salt and black pepper. Cook for 10 minutes more, or until the egg white has turned solid white. Let cool for 10 minutes and then sprinkle each with a few drops of lemon juice before serving.

NOTE: To make this in a baking dish, butter a 9 by 13-inch baking dish or pan. Use the same quantity of ingredients as specified. You don't need to double it despite the use of the larger pan. Proceed as directed.

waffle mac & cheese Serves 6

oven-cooked

Even though this dish is topped with maple syrup–soaked waffles, this actually makes a really great supper because it's light and not too sweet. All you have to do is pour a slightly sweet sparkling white Moscato wine and serve a lightly dressed green salad alongside.

. . . .

- 1 tablespoon kosher salt
- 8 ounces mini farfalle pasta (about 2 cups; or use small elbow macaroni)
- 8 tablespoons (1 stick) salted butter
- 4 waffles (frozen or leftover homemade), cut into ½-inch squares
- ¼ cup plus 2 tablespoons maple syrup, plus more for serving
- 3 large eggs
- 8 ounces fresh goat cheese, at room temperature
- 1 cup ricotta cheese (preferably whole milk), at room temperature and drained if watery
- 4 ounces whole or low-fat cottage cheese
- 3 tablespoons powdered sugar

Preheat the oven to 375°F. Butter an 8-inch square (1½-quart) baking dish or pan (or six 8-ounce ramekins). Set aside.

Fill a 4- to 5-quart pot about three-quarters full with water and add the salt. Bring to a boil and add the pasta. Cook, stirring once or twice, until tender but firm, 4 to 6 minutes, and drain. Reserve the pot.

While the pasta is cooking, in a medium skillet, melt 2 tablespoons of the butter over medium heat. Turn off the heat and add the waffle pieces and ¼ cup of the maple syrup. Stir until mixed well. Set aside.

In a small pot, melt the remaining 6 tablespoons butter. Set aside.

Place the eggs and the remaining 2 tablespoons maple syrup in a large mixing bowl. Using an electric mixer, beat on medium speed until smooth. Add the melted butter, goat cheese, ricotta, and cottage cheese and beat until well incorporated. Stir in the pasta.

Spoon into the prepared baking dish, and top with the waffle pieces. Place the dish on a rimmed baking sheet and bake until the waffles are golden and the casserole is puffy, 50 to 60 minutes. Let cool for 15 minutes. Sprinkle with powdered sugar and serve with more maple syrup alongside.

mushroom, bacon, and eggs mac & cheese Serves 6

oven-cooked

Think of this as mac & cheese meets the omelet. Underneath is the sublime combination of cheese, bacon, and mushrooms; on top is a layer of egg, more cheese, and a little extra bacon for good measure. Note that unlike most of the recipes in this book, this one must be made in a large pan. Otherwise, the eggs will run all over the oven floor.

• •

1 tablespoon plus ½ teaspoon kosher salt, plus more as needed

12 ounces small elbow macaroni

12 slices bacon

1 large yellow or red onion (about 12 ounces), coarsely chopped

1½ pounds white or cremini mushrooms, stemmed and quartered (large ones cut into 6 pieces), or a mix of seasonal mushrooms

2½ teaspoons finely chopped fresh thyme

Freshly ground black pepper

3 tablespoons salted butter

3 tablespoons all-purpose flour

3¾ cups whole or reduced-fat milk

¾ cup heavy cream

1 pound Gruyère cheese, coarsely grated (about 5¼ cups)

½ teaspoon ground or freshly grated nutmeg

4 large eggs

Preheat the oven to 375°F. Butter a 9 by 13-inch (3-quart) baking dish or pan. Set aside.

Fill a 4- to 5-quart pot about three-quarters full with water and add 1 tablespoon of the salt. Bring to a boil and add the pasta. Cook, stirring once or twice, until tender but firm, about 4 minutes, and drain. Reserve the pot.

In a large skillet, cook the bacon until crisp. Transfer to a paper towel–lined plate and crumble into bite-size pieces when cool. Measure out ½ cup of the bacon and set aside. Discard all but about 2 tablespoons of bacon fat from the skillet.

Using the same skillet, cook the onion over medium heat, stirring occasionally, until soft, about 5 minutes. Add the mushrooms and cook until soft and creamy in texture, 6 to 8 minutes. Add the thyme and stir a couple of times. Set aside. When cool, sprinkle with salt and pepper to taste.

Using the same pot you used to cook the pasta, melt the butter over medium heat. Slowly whisk in the flour and stir constantly until a paste forms, 30 to 45 seconds. Continue stirring for about 2 minutes more, or until the mixture starts to darken slightly and smell a bit nutty. Slowly whisk in the milk, cream, and the remaining ½ teaspoon salt and cook until the mixture starts to thicken and is just beginning to bubble around the edges, 5 to 7 minutes. It should be thick enough to coat the back of a wooden spoon. Add 2½ cups of the Gruyère and the nutmeg and cook until the cheese has melted and the sauce is smooth but not too runny. It should be similar in texture to cake batter. If it's soupy, continue cooking until it thickens.

Turn off the heat and add the pasta, the mushroom mixture, and all but the reserved bacon and stir to combine. Pour into the prepared baking dish.

In a medium bowl, whisk the eggs. Season with salt and pepper. Stir in the remaining cheese and pour over the mac & cheese. Sprinkle with the reserved bacon. Place the baking dish on a rimmed baking sheet and bake until bubbling and the cheese is golden brown, about 30 minutes. Let cool for 15 minutes before serving.

spicy "home fries" mac & cheese Serves 6

oven-cooked

To me, the ultimate diner breakfast isn't the eggs you find there, but instead it's the potatoes, especially when they're in the form of home fries. In this mac & cheese, those home-fried potatoes get their just due by acting as the crowning glory on the creamy, cheesy pasta underneath. I don't have to wonder what Dr. Atkins would have said about a potato-on-pasta dish, but this is one splurge worth its weight in carbs.

- -

1 tablespoon plus ½ teaspoon kosher salt, plus more as needed

8 ounces small or medium shell pasta

¼ cup plus 2 tablespoons olive oil

1 pound small red potatoes, cut into ¼-inch chunks (do not peel)

Freshly ground black pepper

1 small onion (about 4 ounces), cut into ½-inch dice

1 medium red bell pepper (about 8 ounces), cut into ½-inch dice

1 medium green bell pepper (about 8 ounces), cut into ½-inch dice

2 teaspoons dried oregano

¼ cup all-purpose flour

1½ cups whole or reduced-fat milk

½ cup heavy cream

12 ounces cheddar cheese, coarsely grated (3½ cups)

2 teaspoons Frank's RedHot Sauce (or use your favorite brand), plus more for serving (use less or more depending on how spicy you want it)

½ teaspoon dry mustard powder

Ketchup, for serving (optional)

Position an oven rack about 6 inches below the broiler and preheat to broil. Butter an 8-inch square (1½-quart) metal pan or six 8-ounce ramekins. Set aside. (Note: Do not use a glass pan or a ceramic dish for this recipe. It can break when set under the broiler.)

Fill a 4- to 5-quart pot about three-quarters full with water and add 1 tablespoon of the salt. Bring to a boil and add the pasta. Cook, stirring once or twice, until tender but firm, 4 to 6 minutes for small shells, 8 to 10 minutes for medium shells, and drain. Reserve the pot.

In a large skillet, heat the ¼ cup of the oil over medium heat. Add the potatoes and cook, stirring occasionally, until the edges are darkened and the potatoes are crisp, 10 to 12 minutes. Add salt and black pepper to taste. Using a slotted spatula or spoon, transfer the potatoes to a plate.

Using the same skillet, cook the onion and bell peppers, stirring occasionally, until the vegetables are soft and beginning to caramelize (darken) around the edges, 8 to 10 minutes. Add the oregano and salt and black pepper to taste. Turn off the heat and set aside.

Using the same pot you used to cook the pasta, heat the remaining 2 tablespoons oil over medium heat. Slowly whisk in the flour and the remaining ½ teaspoon salt and stir constantly until a paste forms, 30 to 45 seconds. Continue stirring for 1 to 2 minutes more, until the mixture starts to darken slightly and smell a bit nutty. Slowly whisk in the milk and cream and stir until the mixture starts to thicken and is just beginning to bubble around the edges, 5 to 7 minutes. It should be thick enough to coat the back of a wooden spoon. Add 3 cups of the cheese, the hot sauce, and mustard powder and stir until the cheese has melted and the sauce is smooth but not too runny. It should be similar in texture to cake batter. If it's soupy, continue cooking until it thickens.

Turn off the heat and add the pasta and peppers. Stir to combine. Transfer the mixture to the prepared dish. Pile the potatoes on top of the casserole and sprinkle the remaining cheese over the potatoes.

Put the pan on a rimmed baking sheet and place under the broiler. Cook until the cheese is bubbly and golden brown and the potatoes that are peeking out begin to darken, 2 to 3 minutes. Watch carefully, because the cheese and potatoes can burn easily. Let cool for 10 to 15 minutes before serving. Pass extra hot sauce and/or ketchup, if desired, alongside.

Add-Ins

Bacon: Cook 8 slices bacon, crumble them, and add along with the pasta and peppers, or

Breakfast sausage links or patties: Brown 8 ounces of sausage, then cut into ½-inch pieces. Add along with the pasta and peppers, and/or

Spinach: Add 6 cups, a handful at a time, along with the pasta and peppers.

huevos rancheros mac & cheese Serves 6

I'll tell you right now that this is not the simplest recipe in the book, but your efforts will unquestionably be rewarded if you make it. The corn tortilla flavor penetrates the entire dish, and the eggs and salsa on top will likely put this recipe at the top of your favorites list. Luckily, there are a few things you can do ahead. First, as with most of the recipes in this book, you can prepare the dish ahead and refrigerate it, leaving the cooking and final egg step until you're ready to serve. Just bring the casserole to room temperature before putting it in the oven. Also, you can make the salsa a day ahead; or even quicker, use your favorite store-bought salsa instead.

. . . .

salsa

6 Roma tomatoes, halved, seeded, and coarsely chopped (or use one 28-ounce can diced tomatoes, drained slightly)

½ small white onion, finely chopped (about ¼ cup)

1 jalapeño chile, stemmed, seeded, and minced

1 small clove garlic, minced

¼ cup packed fresh cilantro leaves, coarsely chopped

1 tablespoon lime juice

1 teaspoon canola oil

Salt and freshly ground black pepper

mac & cheese

1 tablespoon plus 1 teaspoon kosher salt, plus more as needed

8 ounces large elbow macaroni

½ cup plus 2 tablespoons canola or vegetable oil

8 corn tortillas

1 small white onion (about 6 ounces), coarsely chopped (about 1 cup)

1 jalapeño chile, stemmed, seeded, and minced

1 (14.5-ounce) can black beans, drained well

½ cup packed fresh cilantro leaves, coarsely chopped, plus sprigs for garnish (long stems removed)

2 tablespoons all-purpose flour

2 cups whole or reduced-fat milk

1 cup heavy cream

12 ounces medium or sharp cheddar cheese, coarsely grated (about 4 cups)

4 ounces Monterey Jack cheese, coarsely grated (about 1¼ cups)

8 large eggs

1 tablespoon white wine vinegar

1 cup sour cream

For the salsa: In a small bowl, mix together the tomatoes, onion, jalapeño, garlic, cilantro, lime juice, and canola oil. Add salt and black pepper to taste. Let sit for at least 1 hour to allow the flavors to develop. Add more salt and pepper if needed or, if the tomatoes aren't ripe enough, add a touch of sugar if you'd like. (Note: This may be made 1 day ahead and refrigerated.)

For the mac & cheese: Preheat the oven to 375°F. Butter an 8-inch (1½-quart) baking dish or pan (or six 8-ounce ramekins). Set aside.

Fill a 4- to 5-quart pot about three-quarters full with water and add 1 tablespoon of the salt. Bring to a boil and add the pasta. Cook, stirring once or twice, until tender but firm, 4 to 6 minutes, and drain. Reserve the pot.

Line a baking sheet with paper towels. Heat ½ cup of the oil in a medium skillet over medium-high heat. Using tongs, place 1 tortilla in the oil and cook for 1 minute, turning once halfway through. You don't want to crisp it, just to take the raw taste away and heat it through. Place on the prepared baking sheet and continue with the remaining tortillas. Tear the tortillas into quarters. Don't worry if they're not perfect. Discard all but 2 tablespoons oil from the skillet.

Add the onion and jalapeño to the skillet and cook over medium heat, stirring occasionally, until the onion is soft and translucent, about 5 minutes. Stir in the beans and chopped cilantro and cook just until warmed through, about 5 minutes. Add salt to taste.

Using the same pot you used to cook the pasta, heat the remaining 2 table-spoons oil over medium heat. Slowly whisk in the flour and stir constantly until a paste forms, 30 to 45 seconds. Continue stirring for 1 to 2 minutes more, until the mixture starts to darken slightly and smell a bit nutty. Slowly whisk in the milk, cream, and the remaining 1 teaspoon salt and cook until the mixture starts to thicken and is just beginning to bubble around the edges, 5 to 7 minutes. It should be thick enough to coat the back of a wooden spoon. Add 2½ cups of the cheddar and the Monterey Jack and stir until the cheese is melted and the sauce is smooth but not too runny. It should be similar in texture to cake batter. If it's soupy, continue cooking until it thickens.

Turn off the heat and add the pasta and black bean mixture. Stir to combine. Place 8 tortilla pieces on the bottom of the prepared dish, overlapping if necessary. Pour the macaroni mixture into the prepared baking dish. Top with the remaining tortilla pieces and sprinkle with the remaining cheddar. Put the dish on a rimmed baking sheet and bake for 30 minutes, or until the cheese and tortillas are browned and the dish is bubbling. Let cool for 15 minutes.

While the pasta is cooling, poach the eggs: Fill a large bowl about half full with hot water. Set aside. Fill a saucepan with 3 inches of water and 1 teaspoon salt. Bring to a brisk simmer. Do not boil. Stir in the vinegar (this helps hold the egg whites together). Cooking just 2 or 3 at a time, carefully break each egg, one at a time, into a small bowl or ramekin and gently pour the egg into the simmering water. Repeat with the remaining eggs. Cook for about 3 minutes for a runny yolk (longer for a firmer one) and, using a slotted spoon, remove and place in the prepared bowl. If the water has cooled, add more hot water.

To serve, line a plate with paper towels. Spoon out a portion of mac & cheese into a shallow bowl. Using a slotted spoon, lift an egg out of the hot water and blot dry on paper towels. Place on top of the mac & cheese. Sprinkle with salt and pepper and garnish with a cilantro sprig. Pass the sour cream and salsa alongside.

fruit and (mac &) cheese

stovetop

Serves 6

Think of this as the cheese course meets mac & cheese. On a cheese board, often figs, blue cheese, honey, and nuts are featured together, and here they appear together in the comfort of a warm and creamy mac & cheese. Although the dish is on the sweet side, the rosemary creates a magnificent savory note, which is furthered by the smokiness of the crunchy almonds and a sprinkling of coarse salt. As with a cheese board, this mac & cheese is very good at room temperature as well.

- 1 tablespoon plus 1 teaspoon kosher salt
- 8 ounces orecchiette pasta (or use medium shell pasta or large elbow macaroni)
- 2 tablespoons salted butter
- ¼ cup all-purpose flour
- 2 cups whole or reduced-fat milk
- 1 cup heavy cream
- 1 cup mascarpone cheese
- 6 ounces Gorgonzola cheese, coarsely crumbled (or other creamy blue cheese), about ¾ cup
- 2 tablespoons honey
- 1 teaspoon finely chopped fresh rosemary, plus sprigs for garnish (optional)
- ½ teaspoon freshly ground black pepper
- 4 ounces dried figs (12 to 14 figs; preferably Mission), 8 whole figs reserved for garnish, the rest cut into ½-inch pieces

Coarse sea salt, for sprinkling

- ½ cup smoked almonds, coarsely chopped (or use regular almonds, toasted)

Fill a 4- to 5-quart pot about three-quarters full with water and add 1 tablespoon of the salt. Bring to a boil and add the pasta. Cook, stirring once or twice, until tender but firm, about 4 minutes, and drain.

Using the same pot you used to make the pasta, melt the butter over medium heat. Slowly whisk in the flour and stir constantly until a paste forms, 30 to 45 seconds. Continue stirring for about 2 minutes more, or until the mixture starts to darken slightly and smell a bit nutty. Slowly whisk in the milk, cream, and the remaining 1 teaspoon salt and cook until the mixture starts to thicken and is just beginning to bubble around the edges, 5 to 7 minutes. It should be thick enough to coat the back of a wooden spoon. Add the mascarpone; Gorgonzola; honey; rosemary, if desired; and black pepper and stir until the cheese has melted and the sauce is smooth but not too runny. It should be similar in texture to cake batter. If it's soupy, continue cooking until it thickens.

Turn off the heat, add the pasta and chopped figs, and stir to combine. Spoon the mixture into small bowls. Dust with a little coarse sea salt and sprinkle with the almonds. Garnish with 1 whole fig and a rosemary sprig, if desired, and serve.

CHAPTER 6

totally decadent

Smoky Silky Parsnip, Mushroom, and Espresso Mac & Cheese . . . 104

Chicken, Pesto, and Provolone Mac & Cheese . . . 107

Parmesan, Pea, Prosciutto, and Basil Mac & Cheese . . . 110

Butternut Squash, Gruyère, and Brown Butter Mac & Cheese . . . 113

Truffle Mac & Cheese . . . 115

Mediterranean Mac & Cheese . . . 117

Crab, Artichoke, and Swiss Mac & Cheese . . . 119

smoky silky parsnip, mushroom, and espresso mac & cheese Serves 6

Espresso in mac & cheese? The idea for this came after having a delectable pasta at San Francisco's excellent restaurant SPQR. In that dish, chef Matthew Accarino's secret weapon was an espresso-rubbed cheese called Espresso BellaVitano, made by Sartori Cheese in Wisconsin. It's smoky and sweet all at once, and together with the sweet parsnips and smoked mushrooms in the pasta (and not just a little butter), I walked away knowing I'd have to re-create that dish in my own way. And so this mac & cheese, made simpler by using smoked mozzarella instead of smoking the mushrooms, was born. Although the espresso cheese is fairly widely available in stores and online, if you can't find it, use aged Asiago or Parmesan instead.

. . . .

1 tablespoon plus 1 teaspoon salt, plus more as needed

8 ounces penne pasta

5 tablespoons salted butter

2 cups coarse, fresh bread crumbs (preferably homemade)

4 ounces Espresso BellaVitano cheese, finely grated (or Asiago or Parmesan), about 2 cups

1 pound white or cremini mushrooms, stemmed and cut into ½-inch pieces

1½ teaspoons finely chopped fresh thyme

Freshly ground black pepper

8 ounces parsnips (about 4 small), peeled and cut into ½-inch chunks (discard any woody spots)

2 medium cloves garlic, peeled

1½ cups whole or reduced-fat milk

1½ cups heavy cream

8 ounces smoked mozzarella cheese, coarsely grated (or smoked scamorza)

Preheat the oven to 375°F. Butter an 8-inch square (1½-quart) baking dish (or six 8-ounce ramekins). Set aside.

Fill a 4- to 5-quart pot about three-quarters full with water and add 1 tablespoon of the salt. Bring to a boil and add the pasta. Cook, stirring once or twice, until tender but firm, about 8 minutes, and drain. Reserve the pot.

In a medium skillet, melt 2 tablespoons of the butter. Add the bread crumbs and 1 cup of the BellaVitano. Mix well. Transfer to a plate and set aside. Wipe out but do not wash the skillet.

In the same skillet, melt 2 tablespoons of the butter over medium heat. Add the mushrooms and thyme and cook until soft and creamy in texture, 6 to 8 minutes. Let cool slightly and add salt and black pepper to taste. Set aside.

Using the same pot you used to cook the pasta, combine the parsnips, garlic, ½ cup of the milk, ½ cup of the cream, and the remaining 1 tablespoon butter. Cover and cook over low heat, stirring occasionally and watching to make sure the cream mixture does not boil. Simmer the parsnips until they are very soft, 15 to 20 minutes. Cool slightly. Place in a blender or food processor and puree. Put the puree back into the pot, and add the remaining 1 cup milk, 1 cup cream, and 1 teaspoon salt. Cook until slightly thickened and warmed through, about 5 minutes. Add the smoked mozzarella and the remaining BellaVitano, and stir until the sauce is smooth but not too runny. It should be similar in texture to cake batter. If it's soupy, continue cooking until it thickens.

Add the pasta and mushrooms and stir just until mixed. Pour into the prepared baking dish and top with the bread crumb mixture. Place the dish on a rimmed baking sheet and bake for 30 minutes, or until the mixture is brown and bubbly. Let cool for 15 minutes and serve.

chicken, pesto, and provolone mac & cheese Serves 6

oven-cooked

You might look at this recipe and decide there are just too many steps for a mac & cheese. To that, I say the following: 1) You don't feel like making your own pesto? Then by all means buy it! 2) The pesto and the bread crumbs can be made a few days ahead, so you can avoid having to spend a lot of time in the kitchen at once. 3) The explosive flavors of this dish make every step leading up to the finale totally worth it.

pesto

2 cups packed fresh basil leaves, plus sprigs for garnish

2 medium cloves garlic, coarsely chopped

¼ cup pine nuts

4 ounces Parmigiano-Reggiano or Pecorino Romano cheese, finely grated (about 2 cups), plus more for serving

¼ cup extra-virgin olive oil

Salt and freshly ground black pepper

mac & cheese

1 tablespoon plus 1 teaspoon kosher salt, plus more as needed

8 ounces strozzapreti pasta (or use penne or fusilli)

4 (½-inch-wide) slices Italian bread, lightly toasted and cooled, each broken into a few pieces

5 tablespoons extra-virgin olive oil

1 pound boneless, skinless chicken breast, cut into ½-inch pieces

⅛ teaspoon garlic powder

Freshly ground black pepper

2 tablespoons all-purpose flour

2 cups whole or reduced-fat milk

1 cup heavy cream

12 ounces provolone cheese, coarsely grated (about 4 cups)

Preheat the oven to 375°F.

For the pesto: In a blender or food processor, combine the basil, garlic, pine nuts, and 1 cup of the Parmigiano-Reggiano. Blend or process for 45 seconds, or until the mixture is finely chopped. Add the oil and blend just until the pesto is smooth and creamy. Add salt and black pepper to taste. Set aside. (Note: The pesto can be made 2 days in advance, covered with a thin layer of olive oil, and refrigerated; or it can be frozen for up to 1 month.)

For the mac & cheese: Oil an 8-inch square (1½-quart) baking dish or pan (or six 8-ounce ramekins). Set aside.

Fill a 4- to 5-quart pot about three-quarters full with water and add 1 tablespoon of the salt. Bring to a boil and add the pasta. Cook, stirring once or twice, until tender but firm, 6 to 8 minutes, and drain. Reserve the pot.

Put the bread slices in a food processor or blender. Process until the bread is mostly sand-like with a few coarse crumbs, about 45 seconds. (Alternatively, put the bread in a resealable plastic bag and use a rolling pin or other heavy object to crush the bread into crumbs.) In a medium skillet, heat 2 tablespoons of the oil over medium heat. Turn off the heat and add the bread crumbs and the remaining Parmigiano-Reggiano. Stir to combine. Transfer the crumbs to a plate and set aside. Wipe out the skillet with a paper towel but don't wash it.

Place the chicken in a small bowl and sprinkle with the garlic powder and salt and black pepper.

In the same skillet, heat 1 tablespoon of the oil over medium-high heat. Add the chicken and cook, stirring frequently, just until no longer pink, 5 to 7 minutes. Set aside.

Using the same pot you used to cook the pasta, heat the remaining 2 tablespoons olive oil over medium heat. Slowly whisk in the flour and stir constantly until a paste forms, 30 to 45 seconds. Continue stirring for 1 to 2 minutes more, until the mixture starts to darken slightly and smell a bit nutty. Slowly whisk in the milk, cream, and the remaining 1 teaspoon salt and cook until the mixture starts to thicken and is just beginning to bubble around the edges, 5 to 7 minutes. It should be thick enough to coat the back of a wooden spoon. Add 2½ cups of the provolone and cook until the cheese has melted and the sauce is smooth but not too runny. It should be similar in texture to cake batter. If it's soupy, continue cooking just until it begins to thicken.

Add the pasta, chicken, and pesto and stir just to combine. Pour into the prepared baking dish. Sprinkle with the remaining provolone and top with the bread crumb mixture. Place the dish on a rimmed baking sheet and bake until bubbling and golden brown, about 30 minutes. Let cool for 15 minutes before serving.

Add-Ins
Pine nuts: Add ¼ cup pine nuts to the bread crumb mixture.

parmesan, pea, prosciutto, and basil mac & cheese Serves 6

stovetop

This is unquestionably one of my very favorite recipes. I love the freshness of the peas and herbs combined with the richness of the Parmesan cream and prosciutto. Plus, it's a really pretty dish that's also very elegant. Because of that, it's a perfect company dish that is as suitable for a casual evening of entertaining as it is for one using your very best dinnerware.

- 1½ cups whole or reduced-fat milk
- 1½ cups heavy cream
- 2 ounces Parmigiano-Reggiano cheese, coarsely grated (1 cup), plus more for serving
- 1 tablespoon plus 1 teaspoon kosher salt
- 8 ounces orecchiette pasta (or use medium shell pasta)
- 2 tablespoons salted butter
- 2 tablespoons all-purpose flour
- 12 ounces Gruyère cheese, coarsely grated (4 cups)
- ¼ teaspoon freshly ground black pepper, plus more as needed
- ⅛ teaspoon ground or freshly grated nutmeg
- 1½ cups peas, fresh or frozen (no need to defrost if frozen)
- 2 ounces paper-thin slices prosciutto, cut crosswise into ¼-inch-wide strips
- ½ cup fresh basil chiffonade (thin strips), plus sprigs for garnish
- ½ cup fresh mint chiffonade (thin strips)

In a medium saucepan, bring the milk, cream, and half of the Parmesan to a boil (watch carefully so that it doesn't spill over). Turn off the heat and cover the pot for 30 minutes. Strain the mixture into a small bowl and discard the Parmesan. Set aside.

Meanwhile, fill a 4- to 5-quart pot about three-quarters full with water and add 1 tablespoon of the salt. Bring to a boil and add the pasta. Cook, stirring once or twice, until tender but firm, 8 to 10 minutes, and drain.

Using the same pot you used to cook the pasta, melt the butter over medium heat. Slowly whisk in the flour and stir constantly until a paste forms, 30 to 45 seconds. Continue stirring for 1 to 2 minutes, until the mixture starts to darken slightly and smell a bit nutty. Slowly whisk in the Parmesan cream and the remaining 1 teaspoon salt and cook until the mixture starts to thicken and is just beginning to bubble around the edges, 5 to 7 minutes. It should be thick enough to coat the back of a wooden spoon. Add the Gruyère, pepper, and nutmeg and stir until the sauce is smooth but not too runny. It should be similar in texture to cake batter. If it's soupy, continue cooking until it thickens.

Add the pasta, peas, most of the prosciutto (save some for garnish), ¼ cup each of the basil and the mint, and stir until well mixed. Ladle into bowls and top with the remaining chiffonade of basil and the mint and prosciutto strips. Garnish with the whole basil sprigs and serve with extra Parmesan alongside.

butternut squash, gruyère, and brown butter mac & cheese Serves 6

oven-cooked

Ravioli with butternut squash, brown butter, and sage has become a classic fall pasta combination in many upscale restaurants. So why not take it down-home and fold that delectable flavor combination into a mac & cheese? This recipe is a true winner and a dish that your friends and family will love you for, whether you serve it in winter, spring, summer, or fall.

• •

1 tablespoon plus ½ teaspoon kosher salt

8 ounces mini farfalle pasta (or use small elbow macaroni)

5 tablespoons salted butter

2 cups coarse, fresh bread crumbs (preferably homemade)

4 ounces Pecorino Romano or Parmesan cheese, finely grated (about 2 cups)

1 tablespoon finely chopped fresh sage leaves, plus 12 whole leaves

1 pound butternut squash, peeled, seeded, and cut into ½-inch chunks

1½ cups whole or reduced-fat milk

1½ cups heavy cream

12 ounces Gruyère cheese, coarsely grated (about 4 cups)

¼ teaspoon cayenne pepper

Preheat the oven to 375°F. Butter an 8-inch square (1½-quart) baking dish or pan (or six 8-ounce ramekins). Set aside.

Fill a 4- to 5-quart pot about three-quarters full with water and add 1 tablespoon of the salt. Bring to a boil and add the pasta. Cook, stirring once or twice, until tender but firm, 4 to 6 minutes, and drain. Reserve the pot.

In a medium skillet, melt 3 tablespoons of the butter. Turn off the heat and add the bread crumbs and 1 cup of the pecorino. Stir to combine. Transfer to a small bowl and wipe out but do not wash the skillet.

Line a small plate with paper towels. Using the same skillet, melt the remaining 2 tablespoons butter over medium heat and cook just until it's starting to brown. Add the whole sage leaves and cook until the leaves are crisp and just beginning to darken, about 45 seconds. Remove the pan from the heat. Using tongs, transfer the leaves to the paper towel–lined plate and reserve both the leaves and the butter.

Using the same pot you used to cook the pasta, combine the squash, milk, cream, and the remaining ½ teaspoon salt and the reserved sage butter. Cover and cook over medium-low heat, stirring occasionally and watching to make sure the cream mixture does not boil. Simmer the squash until it is very soft, 20 to 25 minutes. Cool slightly. Place about half of the mixture in a blender or food processor and puree. Put the puree back into the pot and repeat with the remaining squash. Add the Gruyère, the remaining pecorino, the chopped sage, and the cayenne to the pureed squash mixture and stir until the cheese has melted (the heat of the squash mixture should melt it). Add the pasta and stir to combine.

Pour into the prepared baking dish, sprinkle with the bread crumb mixture, and place the fried sage leaves in a decorative pattern on top. Place the dish on a rimmed baking sheet and bake for 30 minutes, or until the mixture is brown and bubbly. Let cool for 15 minutes before serving.

Add-Ins

Pancetta: Cut a 4-ounce piece of pancetta into 1-inch long and ¼-inch wide "sticks" or batons. Place in a medium skillet over medium-high heat, and cook until the edges are browned and the pancetta is crisp. Using a slotted spoon, add to the cheese sauce along with the pasta.

truffle mac & cheese Serves 6

It's a sure bet that if a recipe has the word truffle in the title, it's going to be decadent. This dish is no exception, but that doesn't mean it's complicated. It's actually quite easy to make. The important ingredient is the truffle oil, so try not to skimp on the one you buy. Go for the best you can, and you'll be richly rewarded. Likewise, use Italian Fontina if possible for the best results.

- 1 tablespoon plus 1 teaspoon kosher salt
- 8 ounces small shell pasta
- 2 cups coarse, fresh bread crumbs (preferably homemade)
- 1 tablespoon plus 2 teaspoons truffle oil
- 1 tablespoon olive oil
- 2 large eggs, lightly beaten
- 1½ cups whole or reduced-fat milk
- 1½ cups heavy cream
- ½ cup crème fraîche
- Freshly ground black pepper
- ⅛ teaspoon ground or freshly grated nutmeg
- 12 ounces Italian Fontina cheese, coarsely grated (about 4 cups)
- 1 ounce Pecorino Romano or Parmesan cheese, finely grated (about ½ cup)

Preheat the oven to 375°F. Butter an 8-inch square (1½-quart) baking dish or pan (or six 8-ounce ramekins). Set aside.

Fill a 4- to 5-quart pot about three-quarters full with water and add 1 tablespoon of the salt. Bring to a boil and add the pasta. Cook, stirring once or twice, until tender but firm, 4 to 6 minutes, and drain. Reserve the pot.

While the pasta is cooking, put the bread crumbs in a small bowl. Add 1 tablespoon of the truffle oil and the olive oil. Stir to combine.

In a large bowl, whisk together the eggs, milk, cream, crème fraîche, the remaining 2 teaspoons truffle oil, the remaining 1 teaspoon salt, the pepper, and nutmeg. Add the pasta, 2½ cups of the Fontina, and the pecorino. Stir to combine. Pour into the prepared baking dish. Sprinkle with the remaining Fontina and top with the bread crumbs. Place the dish on a rimmed baking sheet and bake until bubbling and golden brown, about 30 minutes. Let cool for 15 minutes before serving.

mediterranean mac & cheese

stovetop

Serves 6

This mac & cheese is decidedly rich and unquestionably delicious. It's creamy, a tad spicy, and has tons of flavor from the lamb and roasted red peppers. Plus, it's versatile. You can take it in a Moroccan direction by adding a small spoonful of the pepper condiment called harissa, found in specialty grocery and Middle Eastern stores. Or you can look toward Spain by adding pimentón, which is a smoked paprika. Then again, it's pretty darned good just as it is. (Did I say it's rich?)

- 1 tablespoon plus ½ teaspoon kosher salt, plus more as needed
- 8 ounces orecchiette pasta (or use large shell pasta)
- ¼ cup olive oil
- 1 medium yellow or red onion (about 8 ounces), coarsely chopped
- 8 ounces ground lamb (or beef)
- 1 (8-ounce) jar roasted red peppers, drained and coarsely chopped
- 1 cup kalamata olives, pitted and coarsely chopped
- 4 ounces feta cheese
- ½ teaspoon red pepper flakes
- Freshly ground black pepper
- 2 tablespoons all-purpose flour
- 1½ cups heavy cream
- 1 cup whole or reduced-fat milk
- 12 ounces Petit Basque cheese, coarsely grated (about 4 cups; or use other Basque-style sheep's milk cheese, a not-too-aged manchego, or Gruyère)

½ cup coarsely chopped fresh Italian parsley, plus 8 sprigs for garnish (long stems removed)

2 ounces ricotta salata cheese, shaved (or use Pecorino Romano)

Fill a 4- to 5-quart pot about three-quarters full with water and add 1 tablespoon of the salt. Bring to a boil and add the pasta. Cook, stirring once or twice, until tender but firm, 10 to 12 minutes, and drain. Reserve the pot.

In a medium skillet, heat 2 tablespoons of the oil over medium-high heat. Add the onion and cook, stirring occasionally, until soft, about 5 minutes. Add the lamb, using a wooden spoon to break it into small pieces, and cook, stirring frequently, until the meat is no longer pink. Add the peppers, olives, feta, and red pepper flakes. Stir just until heated through. Add salt and black pepper to taste. (Keep in mind that the feta and olives are both salty.) Set aside.

Using the same pot you used to cook the pasta, heat the remaining 2 tablespoons oil over medium heat. Slowly whisk in the flour and stir constantly until a paste forms, 30 to 45 seconds. Continue stirring for 1 to 2 minutes more, until the mixture starts to darken slightly and it smells a bit nutty. Slowly whisk in the cream, milk, and the remaining ½ teaspoon salt and cook until the mixture starts to thicken and is just beginning to bubble around the edges, 5 to 7 minutes. It should be thick enough to coat the back of a wooden spoon. Add the Petit Basque and cook until the cheese has melted and the sauce is smooth. Add the pasta, the lamb mixture, and parsley and stir to combine. To serve, ladle the mac & cheese into bowls. Using a vegetable peeler, shave a little ricotta salata over each bowl and sprinkle each with a couple of twists of black pepper. Garnish with the parsley sprigs and serve.

crab, artichoke, and swiss mac & cheese Serves 6

If you've ever eaten crab and artichoke dip, then you'll have a good idea of where this recipe is going. That dip is a classic for a reason, and when it's turned into a mac & cheese, it's even more memorable. Instead of just the jewel on a cracker, the cheesy mixture becomes the crowning glory on a fork, yielding huge gustatory dividends. Note that this dish necessitates a longer wait time between oven and fork than the others in this book. This is because the ingredients simply need a bit more time to marry.

- -

1 tablespoon plus 1 teaspoon kosher salt

8 ounces orecchiette pasta (or use medium shell pasta)

4 tablespoons salted butter

2 cups toasted or stale sourdough bread crumbs

2 ounces Parmigiano-Reggiano or Pecorino Romano cheese, finely grated (about 1 cup)

¾ cup finely diced yellow onion (about ½ medium onion)

2 tablespoons all-purpose flour

1½ cups whole or reduced-fat milk

1½ cups heavy cream

12 ounces Swiss, Jarlsberg, or Gruyère cheese, coarsely grated (about 4 cups)

½ cup ricotta cheese

¼ teaspoon mustard powder

Freshly ground black pepper

2 (6.5-ounce) jars marinated artichoke hearts, drained and cut into ½-inch pieces

8 ounces crabmeat (preferably fresh), picked through for bits of shell

totally decadent 119

Fill a 4- to 5-quart pot about three-quarters full with water and add 1 tablespoon of the salt. Bring to a boil and add the pasta. Cook, stirring once or twice, until tender but firm, 8 to 9 minutes, and drain. Reserve the pot.

While the pasta is cooking, in a medium skillet, melt 2 tablespoons of the butter over medium heat. Turn off the heat and add the bread crumbs and Parmigiano-Reggiano. Stir until combined. Set aside.

Using the same pot you used to cook the pasta, melt the remaining 2 tablespoons butter over medium heat. Add the onion and cook, stirring occasionally, until soft and translucent, about 5 minutes. Slowly whisk in the flour and stir constantly until a paste forms, 30 to 45 seconds. Continue stirring for 1 to 2 minutes more, until the mixture starts to darken slightly and smell a bit nutty. Slowly whisk in the milk, cream, and the remaining 1 teaspoon salt and cook until the mixture starts to thicken and is just beginning to bubble around the edges, 5 to 7 minutes. It should be thick enough to coat the back of a wooden spoon. Add 2½ cups of the Swiss, the ricotta, mustard powder, and black pepper to taste and stir until the sauce is smooth but not too runny. It should be similar in texture to cake batter. If it's soupy, continue cooking until it thickens.

Add the pasta, artichoke hearts, and crabmeat and stir just until combined. Pour into the prepared baking dish. Sprinkle with the remaining cheese and top with the bread crumb mixture. Place the dish on a rimmed baking sheet and bake until bubbling and golden brown, about 30 minutes. Let cool for 20 minutes before serving.

CHAPTER 7

lighten up, cool down

Asparagus, Swiss, and Dill Mac & Cheese . . . 122

Goat Cheese, Mozzarella, Basil, and Tomato
Mac & Cheese . . . 124

Fiery South of the Border Mac & Cheese . . . 127

Light(er) Cheddar and Arugula Mac & Cheese
with Croutons . . . 130

Herbed Zucchini, Havarti, and Whole-Grain
Mac & Cheese . . . 133

asparagus, swiss, and dill mac & cheese Serves 6

stovetop

This is as light and refreshing as a spring day. The dill adds a wonderful zing, and the vegetables make it flavorful and healthy. As with all the recipes in this chapter, feel free to make it a little richer by using regular cheese and/or full-fat milk. But as written, it's good for the taste buds and the waistline.

• •

1 tablespoon plus 1 teaspoon kosher salt, plus more as needed

8 ounces penne pasta (or use medium shell pasta)

3 tablespoons olive oil

1 small onion (about 6 ounces), peeled and cut into ¼-inch pieces

8 ounces medium asparagus spears (5 to 7 spears), ends trimmed, spears cut crosswise into ¼-inch slices, leaving 1-inch tips

2 medium carrots, peeled and cut into ¼-inch dice

2 tablespoons water

2 tablespoons finely chopped fresh dill, plus sprigs, cut into 3-inch pieces, for garnish

Freshly ground black pepper

4 tablespoons all-purpose flour

2 cups reduced or low-fat milk

½ cup skim milk

6 ounces reduced fat Swiss or Jarlsberg cheese, coarsely grated (about 2 cups)

1 cup part-skim ricotta cheese

½ teaspoon dry mustard powder

Fill a 4- to 5-quart pot about three-quarters full with water and add 1 tablespoon of the salt. Bring to a boil and add the pasta. Cook, stirring once or twice, until tender but firm, about 4 minutes, and drain. Reserve the pot.

In a medium skillet, heat 1 tablespoon of the oil over medium-high heat. Add the onion, asparagus, carrots, and water and cook until the vegetables are tender, 7 to 8 minutes. Add the chopped dill and salt and pepper to taste. Set aside.

Using the same pot you used to cook the pasta, heat the remaining 2 tablespoons oil over medium heat. Slowly whisk in the flour and stir constantly until a paste forms, 30 to 45 seconds. Continue stirring for 1 to 2 minutes more, until the mixture starts to darken slightly and smell a bit nutty. Lower the heat to medium-low. Slowly add the milks and the remaining 1 teaspoon salt and cook until the mixture is just beginning to thicken and bubble around the edges, 5 to 7 minutes. It should be thick enough to coat the back of a wooden spoon. Add the cheeses and mustard powder and cook until smooth but not runny. It should be similar in texture to cake batter. If it's soupy, continue cooking until it thickens.

Add the pasta and vegetables and stir to combine. Ladle into bowls and garnish with the dill sprigs. Serve right away.

goat cheese, mozzarella, basil, and tomato mac & cheese

stovetop

Serves 6

This recipe celebrates summer's favorite trio: tomatoes, basil, and mozzarella. The added twist is the lemon zest, which makes it ultra-refreshing. Best of all, you get lots of flavor in this mac & cheese even though it's made mostly with skim milk. Talk about the perfect combo!

- -

1 tablespoon plus ½ teaspoon kosher salt

8 ounces small conchiglie (shell) pasta (or use small elbow macaroni)

1 tablespoon salted butter

1 tablespoon olive oil, plus more for drizzling

¼ cup all-purpose flour

2 cups skim milk

½ cup reduced- or low-fat milk

4 ounces fresh goat cheese, coarsely crumbled (about ¾ cup)

6 ounces part-skim mozzarella cheese, coarsely grated (about 2 cups)

¾ cup coarsely chopped fresh basil, plus 8 leaves for garnish

2 teaspoons finely chopped lemon zest

1½ cups halved cherry tomatoes

1 ounce Parmesan cheese, finely grated

Freshly ground black pepper

Fill a 4- to 5-quart pot about three-quarters full with water and add 1 tablespoon of the salt. Bring to a boil and add the pasta. Cook, stirring once or twice, until tender but firm, 4 to 6 minutes, and drain.

Using the same pot you used to cook the pasta, heat the butter and oil over medium heat. Slowly whisk in the flour and stir constantly until a paste forms, 30 to 45 seconds. Continue stirring for 1 to 2 minutes more, until the mixture starts to darken slightly and smell a bit nutty. Turn heat to medium-low. Slowly whisk in the milks and the remaining ½ teaspoon salt and cook until the mixture is hot and just beginning to bubble around the edges, 5 to 7 minutes. It should be thick enough to coat the back of a wooden spoon. Add the cheeses, the chopped basil, and lemon zest and stir until the sauce is smooth but not runny. It should be similar in texture to cake batter. If it's soupy, continue cooking until it thickens.

Add the pasta and half the tomatoes and stir just until mixed in. Ladle into bowls and top with the remaining tomatoes. Sprinkle with the Parmesan and black pepper. Garnish with the basil leaves and serve right away.

fiery south of the border mac & cheese Serves 6

stovetop

This mac & cheese is not for the faint of heart. It's definitely spicy. But it's easy to tone down if you wish. All you need to do is use a little less chile, cut back on the amount of pickled jalapeño, and use a combination of pepper Jack and regular Monterey Jack. No matter what, cream and spice of any level in the same bite is an unbeatable combination. Although the salsa in this recipe is easy to make, if it's too hot to turn on the oven, or you can't find tomatillos or don't have the time to make it, then use purchased green salsa.

• •

salsa

> 8 ounces tomatillos, husks removed and quartered
>
> 1 medium white or yellow onion (about 8 ounces), peeled and cut lengthwise into 6 pieces
>
> 1 serrano chile, halved lengthwise and seeded
>
> 2 tablespoons canola or vegetable oil
>
> ½ teaspoon kosher salt, plus more as needed
>
> Freshly ground black pepper to taste
>
> ¼ cup coarsely chopped fresh cilantro leaves
>
> 2 tablespoons water

mac & cheese

> 1 tablespoon plus 1 teaspoon kosher salt, plus more as needed
>
> 8 ounces small elbow macaroni
>
> 2 tablespoons canola or vegetable oil
>
> ¼ cup all-purpose flour
>
> 2 cups reduced fat milk

½ cup skim milk

12 ounces low-fat pepper Jack cheese, coarsely grated (3½ cups)

¾ cup corn kernels, fresh or frozen (no need to thaw if frozen)

2 whole pickled jalapeño chiles, finely chopped

½ cup coarsely chopped fresh cilantro leaves, plus sprigs for garnish

½ cup low-fat sour cream

For the salsa: Preheat the oven to 375°F. Put the tomatillos, onion, and chile on a large rimmed baking sheet. Drizzle with the oil. Sprinkle with the salt and a little black pepper. Roast the vegetables, stirring occasionally, until the tomatillos have collapsed, about 20 minutes. Let cool slightly. Put in a food processor or blender with the cilantro and water and process until smooth. Taste and add more salt if necessary. Set aside. (Note: This can be made up to 2 days ahead, covered, and refrigerated.)

For the mac & cheese: Fill a 4- to 5-quart pot about three-quarters full with water and add 1 tablespoon of the salt. Bring to a boil and add the pasta. Cook until tender but firm, 4 to 6 minutes, and drain.

Using the same pot you used to cook the pasta, heat the oil over medium heat. Slowly whisk in the flour and stir constantly until a paste forms, 30 to 45 seconds. Continue whisking for 1 to 2 minutes more, until the mixture starts to darken slightly and smell a bit nutty. Turn heat to medium-low. Slowly whisk in the milks and the remaining 1 teaspoon salt and cook until the mixture starts to thicken and is just beginning to bubble around the edges, 5 to 7 minutes. It should be thick enough to coat the back of a wooden spoon. Add the cheese and stir until melted and the sauce is smooth but not runny. It should be similar in texture to cake batter. If it's soupy, continue cooking, stirring constantly, until it thickens.

Add the pasta, corn, jalapeños, and cilantro and stir to combine. Ladle into bowls. Top with a couple of spoonfuls of salsa and dollop with a small spoonful of sour cream. Garnish with the whole cilantro sprigs and serve right away.

Add-Ins

Black beans: Add ½ cup cooked black beans, drained if canned, along with the pasta, and/or

Chicken: Cut 1 pound boneless, skinless chicken breasts into bite-size pieces. Cook in a medium skillet over medium heat, stirring constantly, until no longer pink, 5 to 7 minutes. Season with salt, black pepper, and a little cumin if desired. Using a slotted spoon, add along with the pasta and other ingredients.

light(er) cheddar and arugula mac & cheese with croutons Serves 6

stovetop

When the weather is hot but you still want something cheesy, this is the perfect go-to recipe. It's light because of the lower-fat cheese and milk, and it's also refreshing because of the arugula, which is added just before serving. Best of all, the mini croutons add the necessary crunch without adding a lot of calories.

• •

1 tablespoon plus 1 teaspoon kosher salt, plus more as needed

8 ounces small elbow macaroni

3 tablespoons olive oil

2 sandwich-size slices sourdough bread, crusts removed and cut into ¼-inch cubes

½ medium onion (about 4 ounces), finely chopped

¼ cup all-purpose flour

2 cups skim milk

½ cup reduced- or low-fat milk

12 ounces reduced-fat cheddar cheese, coarsely grated (preferably orange; about 4 cups)

½ teaspoon cayenne pepper

½ teaspoon mustard powder

6 cups arugula leaves (about 6 ounces)

Freshly ground black pepper

Fill a 4- to 5-quart pot about three-quarters full with water and add 1 tablespoon of the salt. Bring to a boil and add the pasta. Cook, stirring once or twice, until tender but firm, about 4 minutes, and drain. Reserve the pot.

In a medium nonstick skillet, heat 1 tablespoon of the oil over medium-high heat. Add the bread cubes and cook, stirring frequently, until they are browned and lightly toasted, about 10 minutes. Set the croutons aside.

Using the same pot you used to cook the pasta, heat the remaining 2 tablespoons oil over medium heat. Add the onion and cook, stirring occasionally, until soft and translucent, about 5 minutes. Slowly whisk in the flour and stir constantly until the onion is coated with the flour, 30 to 45 seconds. Continue stirring for 1 to 2 minutes more, until the mixture starts to darken slightly and smell a bit nutty. Turn the heat to medium-low. Slowly add the milks and the remaining 1 teaspoon salt and stir until the mixture is just beginning to thicken and bubble around the edges, 5 to 7 minutes. It should be thick enough to coat the back of a wooden spoon. Add the cheese, cayenne, and mustard powder and cook, stirring constantly, until smooth but not runny. It should be similar in texture to cake batter. If it's soupy, continue cooking until it thickens.

Add the pasta and stir to combine. Add the arugula in large handfuls, stirring until it wilts a little before adding more. Season with black pepper to taste. Ladle into bowls and top with the croutons. Serve right away.

Add-Ins

Oven-roasted tomatoes (page 16): Add a batch of the tomatoes just before adding the arugula, and/or

Bacon: Cook and crumble 8 slices bacon. Add just before adding the arugula, and/or

Fresh goat cheese: Add 4 ounces crumbled goat cheese along with the cheddar.

herbed zucchini, havarti, and whole-grain mac & cheese

Serves 6

The fresh herbs in this dish really make it sing. Feel free to mix up or even add to those herbs, though. Fresh mint, oregano, and marjoram are all good candidates. Note that when using reduced-fat cheese, it's important to cook the mixture slowly. Otherwise, the cheese may clump. If that happens, then add a couple of teaspoons of flour and stir. The sauce should smooth out.

- 1 tablespoon plus ½ teaspoon kosher salt, plus more as needed
- 8 ounces whole-grain rotini pasta (or use whole-grain fusilli)
- ¼ cup olive oil
- 1 clove garlic, minced
- 1 bunch scallions (8 to 10), white and light green parts only, coarsely chopped
- 2 medium zucchini (about 6 ounces each), cut into ¼-inch cubes
- ¼ cup coarsely chopped fresh basil leaves
- ¼ cup coarsely chopped fresh tarragon leaves
- Freshly ground black pepper
- ¼ cup all-purpose flour
- 1½ cups skim milk
- 1 cup reduced- or low-fat milk
- 12 ounces reduced fat Havarti cheese, coarsely grated (about 4 cups)
- 1 recipe oven-roasted tomatoes (2 cups), (page 16)
- 2 ounces aged Asiago cheese, finely grated (or use Parmesan)

Fill a 4- to 5- quart pot about three-quarters full with water and add 1 tablespoon of the salt. Bring to a boil and add the pasta. Cook, stirring once or twice, until tender but firm, 6 to 8 minutes, and drain. Reserve the pot.

In a medium skillet, heat 2 tablespoons of the oil over medium heat. Add the garlic and half the scallions and cook for 2 minutes, stirring constantly. Add the zucchini and cook, stirring occasionally, until bright green and tender but still firm, 5 to 7 minutes. Add the basil, tarragon, and salt and pepper to taste. Set aside.

Using the same pot you used to cook the pasta, heat the remaining 2 table-spoons oil over medium heat. Slowly whisk in the flour and stir constantly until a paste forms, 30 to 45 seconds. Continue stirring for 1 to 2 minutes more, until the mixture starts to darken slightly and smell a bit nutty. Turn heat to medium-low. Slowly whisk in the milks and the remaining ½ teaspoon salt and cook until the mixture is hot and just beginning to bubble around the edges, 5 to 7 minutes. It should be thick enough to coat the back of a wooden spoon. Add the cheese and stir until the sauce is smooth but not runny. It should be similar in texture to cake batter. If it's soupy, continue cooking until it thickens.

Add the pasta, the zucchini mixture, and tomatoes and stir to combine. Ladle into bowls. Sprinkle with the Asiago and top with the remaining scallions.

CHAPTER 8

party time

Mad Men Mac & Cheese . . . 136

Pizza Mac & Cheese with Ciabatta Croutons . . . 139

Ellen's Noodle Kugel . . . 142

Buffalo Chicken and Crispy Skin Mac & Cheese . . . 144

"Paella" Mac & Cheese . . . 148

Nacho Mac & Cheese . . . 150

mad men mac & cheese Serves 12 to 16

oven-cooked

I will be the first to admit that this recipe seems a bit wacky. Green olives? Gin? Velveeta? Saltines? Really? But wait till you try it. Even if you weren't living in the 1960s (or are not a *Mad Men* watcher), it may very well make you nostalgic for that bygone era. The television show may have been the inspiration for this, but the enduring appeal of a super rich yet retro mac & cheese unquestionably makes it a dish for today's tastes.

· ·

2 tablespoons plus 2 teaspoons kosher salt

1 pound small elbow macaroni

6 tablespoons salted butter

2 cups crushed saltine crackers

¼ cup all-purpose flour

4 cups reduced-fat milk

1 pound Velveeta, cut into 1-inch cubes (or use Cheddar, coarsly grated)

½ cup gin

½ teaspoon cayenne pepper

¼ teaspoon freshly ground black pepper

¼ teaspoon mustard powder

1½ cups pimiento-stuffed green olives, well drained and coarsely chopped

8 ounces cream cheese, cut into ½-inch pieces

Preheat the oven to 375°F. Butter a 9 by 13-inch baking dish or pan. Set aside.

Fill a 6- to 8-quart pot about three-quarters full with water and add 2 tablespoons of the salt. Bring to a boil and add the pasta. Cook, stirring once or twice, until tender but firm, about 4 minutes, and drain. Reserve the pot.

While the pasta is cooking, melt 2 tablespoons of the butter in a medium skillet. Add the saltines and stir to coat. Set aside.

Using the same pot you used to cook the pasta, melt the remaining 4 tablespoons butter over medium heat. Slowly whisk in the flour and stir constantly until a paste forms, 30 to 45 seconds. Continue stirring for about 2 minutes more, or until the mixture starts to darken slightly and smell a bit nutty. Add the milk and the remaining 2 teaspoons of salt and cook until the mixture starts to thicken and is just beginning to bubble around the edges, 5 to 7 minutes. It should be thick enough to coat the back of a wooden spoon. Add the Velveeta, gin, cayenne, black pepper, and mustard powder and stir until the cheese is melted and the sauce is smooth but not too runny. It should be similar in texture to cake batter. If it's soupy, continue cooking until it thickens.

Add the pasta and olives and stir to combine. Pour the mixture into the prepared pan. Dot with the cream cheese and sprinkle with the saltines. Place the dish on a rimmed baking sheet and bake until bubbling and golden brown, 25 to 30 minutes. Let cool for 15 to 20 minutes before serving.

Add-Ins
Potato chips: Swap out the saltines for 4 cups crushed potato chips, and/or **Black Forest ham:** Cut a 6-ounce piece into bite-size pieces and add along with the pasta.

pizza mac & cheese with ciabatta croutons

oven-cooked

Serves 12 to 16

What's better for a party than pizza? Why, a pizza mac & cheese, of course! This recipe features the ingredients from the best of the old-fashioned pizzas—pepperoni, mushrooms, and olives—and bathes them in a creamy mozzarella sauce. But you can customize the recipe to echo the flavors in your own favorite pizza.

. . . .

2 tablespoons plus 2 teaspoons kosher salt, plus more as needed

1 pound large elbow macaroni

4 ciabatta rolls, cut into 3-inch-wide pieces (or use 1 ciabatta loaf or Italian bread, cut into ½-inch cubes)

3 ounces pecorino cheese, finely grated (about 1½ cups)

½ cup plus 2 tablespoons olive oil

2 pounds cremini or white mushrooms, stems removed and quartered (larger mushrooms cut into 6 pieces)

1 tablespoon dried oregano

Freshly ground black pepper

¼ cup all-purpose flour

4 cups whole or reduced-fat milk

2 cups heavy cream

1 ½ pounds fresh mozzarella cheese, thinly sliced

8 ounces pepperoni, cut into ¼-inch cubes (if using pre-sliced pepperoni, then coarsely chopped)

2 recipes oven-roasted tomatoes (4 cups), (page 16)

2 cups kalamata olives, pitted and coarsely chopped

¾ teaspoon red pepper flakes

Preheat the oven to 375°F. Butter a 9 by 13-inch (3-quart) baking dish or pan (or sixteen 8-ounce ramekins). Set aside.

Fill a 6- to 8-quart pot about three-quarters full with water and add 2 tablespoons of the salt. Bring to a boil and add the pasta. Cook, stirring once or twice, until tender but firm, about 4 minutes, and drain. Reserve the pot.

Place the ciabatta cubes and ¾ cup of the pecorino in a large bowl. Drizzle with ¼ cup of the olive oil and stir to mix. Set aside.

Heat 2 tablespoons of the oil in a large nonstick skillet over medium heat. Add the mushrooms and cook stirring occasionally, until soft, 5 to 7 minutes. Add the oregano and season with salt and black pepper to taste. Set aside.

Using the same pot you used to cook the pasta, heat the remaining ¼ cup oil over medium heat. Slowly whisk in the flour and stir constantly until a paste forms, 30 to 45 seconds. Continue stirring for about 2 minutes more, or until the mixture starts to darken slightly and smell a bit nutty. Slowly whisk in the milk, cream, and the remaining 2 teaspoons salt and cook until the mixture starts to thicken and is just beginning to bubble around the edges, 5 to 7 minutes. It should be thick enough to coat the back of a wooden spoon. Add 6 cups of the mozzarella and the remaining pecorino. Stir until the cheese has melted and the sauce is smooth but not too runny. It should be similar in texture to cake batter. If it's soupy, continue cooking until it thickens.

Add the pasta, mushrooms, pepperoni, tomatoes, olives, and red pepper flakes and stir to combine. Pour into the prepared baking dish. Sprinkle with the remaining mozzarella and top with the ciabatta cubes. Place the dish on a rimmed baking sheet and bake until bubbling and golden brown, about 30 minutes. Let cool for 15 to 20 minutes before serving.

Add-Ins

Green bell peppers: Cut 1 large green bell pepper lengthwise into strips, and cut those strips into thirds. Add along with the mushrooms, pepperoni, and olives, or

Roasted red peppers: Coarsely chop 1 cup of jarred roasted red peppers and add along with the mushrooms, pepperoni, and olives, and/or

Roasted garlic: Cut off the top of a bulb of garlic, about 1/4 inch from the end. Brush with olive oil and wrap in aluminum foil. Roast in the oven for about 45 minutes, or until the cloves are soft and creamy. Squeeze the creamy cloves out of their skin into the cheese sauce along with the mushrooms, pepperoni, and olives.

ellen's noodle kugel

Serves 12 to 16

When I told former Aspen restaurant owner Ellen Walbert that I was writing a book about mac & cheese, she asked whether or not there would be a kugel recipe in the book. I told her that that was my plan, but that I wasn't very good at making the traditional touch-of-sweet noodle dish myself. She came to the rescue with her kugel recipe, which has a head-scratchingly light texture (with all that dairy?) and is not too sweet. If you like your kugel sweeter, add 1/4 cup sugar to the cheese mixture. Sweet or not, this is definitely the best kugel I've ever had. (Sorry, Mom!)

2 cups cornflakes, lightly crushed

½ cup plus 2 tablespoons sugar

½ teaspoon ground cinnamon

5 teaspoons kosher salt

1 pound extra-wide egg noodles

10 tablespoons (1¼ sticks) unsalted butter, cut in pieces

8 ounces cream cheese, at room temperature

6 large eggs

16 ounces regular or low-fat cottage cheese

2 cups sour cream

2 teaspoons vanilla extract

1 cup golden raisins or dried cherries (optional)

Preheat the oven to 350°F. Butter a 9 by 13-inch baking dish or pan. Set aside.

In a small bowl, mix together the cornflakes, 2 tablespoons of the sugar, and the cinnamon. Set aside.

Fill a 6- to 8 -quart pot about three-quarters full with water and add 4½ teaspoons of the salt. Bring to a boil and add the noodles. Cook until tender but firm, about 7 minutes. Drain well and return the pasta to the warm pot. Add 8 tablespoons (1 stick) of the butter, tossing until the noodles are well coated.

Place the remaining ½ cup sugar, the cream cheese, and eggs in a large bowl. With an electric mixer, beat on medium speed until smooth. Add the cottage cheese, sour cream, vanilla, and the remaining ½ teaspoon salt and beat until well incorporated. Stir in the raisins, if desired.

Add the egg mixture to the noodles in the pan and stir until well mixed. Spoon into the prepared baking dish and sprinkle with the topping. Dot with the remaining 2 tablespoons butter. Bake for 50 to 60 minutes, until the kugel is set and the topping and edges are golden brown. Let cool for 15 to 20 minutes before serving.

buffalo chicken and crispy skin mac & cheese

Serves 12 to 16

While it wouldn't be too smart to put actual chicken wings in mac & cheese, I discovered it's pretty easy to replicate the flavors found in the popular snack in a mac & cheese. The key is, of course, lots of hot sauce and the signature blue cheese. But wings are often crispy, so my answer to that is to top the casserole with crisped chicken skin. It's easy to make and, because of its potato chip–like texture, totally addictive. After that, the dish is open to interpretation. But needless to say, this recipe has lots of cheese! If you have leftovers, this dish makes particularly good fried bites (see page 21).

· ·

chicken and crispy skin

    2 pounds skin-on, boneless chicken breasts (about 4 halves; see Note)

    2 tablespoons salted butter

    ¼ cup Frank's RedHot Sauce or Frank's RedHot Buffalo Wings Sauce (or use your favorite brand)

    1 teaspoon salt

    Freshly ground black pepper

mac & cheese

    2 tablespoons plus 2 teaspoons kosher salt

    1 pound small shell pasta (or use small elbow macaroni)

    4 tablespoons salted butter

    ¼ cup all-purpose flour

    4 cups whole or reduced-fat milk

    2 cups heavy cream

1½ pounds unaged Gouda or cheddar, coarsely grated (about 8 cups)

8 ounces creamy blue cheese, crumbled (about 1½ cups)

8 ounces cream cheese, cut into ½-inch pieces

¾ cup Frank's RedHot Sauce, plus more for a super-fiery mac & cheese (or use your favorite brand)

1 teaspoon mustard powder

8 medium celery stalks, cut into ¼-inch dice (about 2½ cups)

¾ cup finely chopped fresh chives

For the chicken: Carefully remove the skin in one piece. Set aside. Cut the meat into ½-inch pieces. Melt the butter in a large skillet over medium-high heat. Add the chicken and cook, stirring occasionally, until the meat is no longer pink. Using a slotted spoon, transfer to a large bowl. Add the hot sauce and stir to combine. Wipe out the skillet with a paper towel but do not wash it.

For the crispy skin: Add the reserved chicken skin to the same skillet, and cook over medium-high heat until the undersides are golden brown, about 5 minutes. Use a spatula to flatten the skin if it begins to curl. You want to get the skin as bubble-free and paper-thin as possible. Turn and cook the other side until golden brown and very crisp, 5 to 7 minutes. Watch carefully, because it can burn easily. Season with the salt and pepper to taste. Place on a paper towel–lined plate, where the skin will continue to crisp as it cools. When cool, break into bite-size pieces. Set aside. (Note: The crispy skin can be made up to 2 days ahead and stored in an airtight container.)

For the mac & cheese: Preheat the oven to 375°F. Butter a 9 by 13-inch (3-quart) baking dish or pan (or twelve 8-ounce ramekins). Set aside.

Fill a 6- to 8-quart pot about three-quarters full with water and add 2 tablespoons of the salt. Bring to a boil and add the pasta. Cook, stirring once or twice, until tender but firm, about 4 minutes, and drain.

Using the same pot you used to cook the pasta, melt the butter over medium heat. Slowly whisk in the flour and stir constantly until a paste forms, 30 to 45 seconds. Continue stirring for about 2 minutes more, or until the mixture starts to darken slightly and smell a bit nutty. Slowly whisk in the milk, cream, and the remaining 2 teaspoons salt and cook until the mixture starts to thicken and just beginning to bubble around the edges, 5 to 7 minutes. It should be thick enough to coat the back of a wooden spoon. Add 6 cups of the Gouda, the blue cheese, cream cheese, hot sauce, and mustard powder. Stir until the cheese has melted and the sauce is smooth but not too runny. It should be similar in texture to cake batter. If it's soupy, continue cooking until it thickens.

Add the pasta, chicken, celery, and chives and stir to combine. Pour into the prepared baking dish. Sprinkle the remaining Gouda on top, and top with the crispy skin pieces. Place the dish on a rimmed baking sheet and bake until bubbling and golden brown, about 30 minutes. Let cool for 15 to 20 minutes before serving.

NOTE: Some chicken breasts seem to have more skin than others. If yours doesn't have much skin, buy 1 or 2 more breasts or even a whole chicken, depending on how much you love crispy skin. Remove the skin (an admittedly tricky task when it's a whole chicken) and cook it as directed. Save the meat for another use.

Add-Ins
Pancetta: Cut a 6-ounce piece into bite-size pieces. Cook in a medium skillet over medium-high heat until browned around the edges. Drain on paper towels and add along with the chicken.

"paella" mac & cheese

Serves 12 to 16

This mac & cheese is based very loosely on Spain's national dish, paella. But unlike that dish, this one has cheese (three cheeses, to be precise!), which is a great foil for the traditional spicy chorizo. While paella is known for the crust that forms on the bottom of the pan, the crunch in this dish comes from the addictive cheese crisps that go on top. You may want to make a few extra for snacking.

- 1 pound manchego cheese (preferably aged), coarsely grated (about 5¼ cups)
- 2 tablespoons plus 2 teaspoons salt
- 1 pound small conchiglie (shell) pasta
- 4 tablespoons salted butter
- ¼ cup all-purpose flour
- 5 cups whole or reduced-fat milk
- 1 pound Spanish blue cheese (such as Cabrales), coarsely crumbled (or use Gorgonzola, about 3 cups)
- 8 ounces fresh goat cheese (about 1 ½ cups)
- 8 ounces cooked hot Spanish chorizo, cut into roughly ¼-inch size pieces (see Note)
- 8 ounces cooked baby shrimp
- 1½ cups fresh or frozen peas (no need to defrost if frozen)
- Freshly ground black pepper

Preheat the oven to 375°F.

Line 2 baking sheets with parchment paper or silicone baking mats. Measure out 2 cups of Manchego.

To make the cheese crisps, measure 2 tablespoons of the manchego. Make a shallow pile with the cheese on a baking sheet and smooth into a 2½-inch round. Continue with the remaining cheese, spacing the piles about 3 inches apart. Place in the oven and bake for 8 to 10 minutes, until deep golden brown. Let cool for 5 minutes. Use a spatula to loosen the cheese crisps. Set the cheese crisps aside to cool completely. Makes about 16 crisps.

Fill a 6- to 8-quart pot about three-quarters full with water and add 2 tablespoons of the salt. Bring to a boil and add the pasta. Cook, stirring once or twice, until tender but firm, 4 to 6 minutes. Drain well.

Using the same pot, melt the butter over medium heat. Slowly whisk in the flour and stir constantly until a paste forms, 30 to 45 seconds. Continue stirring for about 2 minutes more, or until the mixture starts to darken slightly and smell a bit nutty. Slowly whisk in the milk and the remaining 2 teaspoons salt and cook until the mixture starts to thicken and is just beginning to bubble around the edges, 5 to 7 minutes. It should be thick enough to coat the back of a wooden spoon. Add the remaining manchego, the blue cheese, and goat cheese and cook until the cheese has melted and the sauce is smooth but not too runny. It should be similar in texture to cake batter. If it's soupy, continue cooking until it thickens.

Add the pasta, chorizo, shrimp, and peas and stir until combined and the peas are cooked through, about 5 minutes. Add the black pepper to taste. Ladle into bowls. Insert a cheese crisp just deep enough so that it will stand straight up. Serve right away.

NOTE: Spanish chorizo is smoked and almost always precooked, while Mexican chorizo has completely different spices and is almost always sold raw. You can find Spanish chorizo in many specialty grocery stores or online at www.tienda.com.

nacho mac & cheese Serves 12 to 16

You guessed it. For this recipe, the tried-and-true football-watching snack is transformed into a tasty mac & cheese. The main difference (besides the inclusion of pasta, of course) is that instead of the chips serving as the foundation for the nachos, they create a super-crunchy topping. But don't worry—as you'll see, they still have the requisite melted cheese on top. The rest of the ingredients remain loyal to the dish's inspiration. Feel free to add your own favorite nacho flavor twist, though.

. . . .

12 ounces tortilla chips

2 tablespoons plus 2 teaspoons kosher salt

1 pound small shell pasta

¼ cup canola or vegetable oil

1 large red onion (about 12 ounces), coarsely chopped (about 2 cups)

¼ cup all-purpose flour

4 cups whole or reduced-fat milk

2 cups heavy cream

1 pound sharp cheddar cheese, coarsely grated (about 5¼ cups)

8 ounces pepper Jack cheese, coarsely grated (about 2½ cups)

1½ cups sour cream

1 cup sliced black olives

1 cup coarsely chopped fresh cilantro leaves, plus sprigs for garnish

¼ cup canned or jarred jalapeño chiles, finely chopped

½ teaspoon cayenne pepper

4 ounces queso fresco, crumbled (or use feta)

1 cup salsa (page 127; or use store-bought)

Guacamole (recipe follows)

Preheat the oven to 375°F. Butter a 9 by 13-inch (3-quart) baking dish or pan. Set aside.

Place the tortilla chips in the bowl of a food processor and pulse just until the chips are coarse, not sand-like. (Alternatively, put the tortilla chips in a large resealable plastic bag and use a rolling pin or other heavy object to crush the chips.) Set aside.

Fill a 6- to 8-quart pot about three-quarters full with water and add 2 tablespoons of the salt. Bring to a boil and add the pasta. Cook, stirring once or twice, until tender but firm, about 4 minutes, and drain.

Using the same pot you used to cook the pasta, heat the oil over medium heat. Add the onion and cook for 5 minutes, or until soft. Slowly whisk in the flour and stir constantly until the onion is coated with the flour, 30 to 45 seconds. Continue stirring for 1 to 2 minutes more, until the mixture starts to darken slightly and smell a bit nutty. Slowly whisk in the milk, cream, and the remaining 2 teaspoons salt and cook until the mixture starts to thicken and is just beginning to bubble around the edges, 5 to 7 minutes. It should be thick enough to coat the back of a wooden spoon. Add 3 cups of the cheddar and the pepper Jack and stir until the sauce is smooth but not too runny. It should be similar in texture to cake batter. If it's soupy, continue cooking until it thickens.

Add the pasta, ½ cup of the sour cream, the olives, chopped cilantro, jalapeños, and cayenne. Pour into the prepared baking dish. Top with the crushed tortillas, and sprinkle with the remaining cheddar. Put the dish on a rimmed baking sheet and bake until bubbling and golden brown, about 30 minutes.

Remove from the oven and sprinkle with the queso fresco. Let cool for 15 to 20 minutes. To serve, garnish each serving with a cilantro sprig. Pass the salsa, guacamole, and the remaining 1 cup sour cream alongside.

guacamole   Makes about 1 cup

1 ripe avocado (preferably Hass)

1 tablespoon fresh lime juice

½ teaspoon kosher salt, plus more as needed

2 tablespoons coarsely chopped onion

2 tablespoons coarsely chopped fresh cilantro

1 teaspoon canned or jarred jalapeño chile, finely chopped

Split and pit the avocado, scoop out the flesh, and mash it in a medium bowl with the lime juice and salt, using a potato masher or fork. Do not use a blender or food processor. You want to keep the avocado slightly chunky, not make it soupy. Stir in the onion, cilantro, and chile. Let sit for about 15 minutes to allow the flavors to meld. Taste, and add more salt if necessary. (Note: You can make this a couple of hours ahead. Just drizzle the surface generously with lime juice to prevent it from browning and refrigerate until ready to use.)

Add-Ins

Rotisserie chicken: Cut 1½ pounds cooked rotisserie chicken into bite-size pieces. Add along with the pasta. Alternatively, shred the chicken and use to top each serving.

acknowledgments

As with all my books, this one was a team effort. Never mind the fact only my name appears on the cover. I have a bevy of people I consider "coauthors." Their names are here because their imprint on this book is indelible.

To Carole Bidnick, my agent, who not only nurtured this, my sixth cheese project, but who also has shown extraordinary kindness and compassion toward me in areas extending far beyond cheese. For her, there are no words. To my editor Jean Lucas, who's casual in style but eagle-eyed in her work. And funny, too! And to the rest of the exemplary Andrews McMeel team—publicist Tammie Barker, publisher Kirsty Melville, designer Julie Barnes, and sales VP extraordinaire Lynne McAdoo, I thank you.

Were it not for cookbook author, recipe-tester, and North Carolina funny gene carrier Sheri Castle, the recipes in this book would be good—just not great. She took my recipes and, as always, applied her expertise, spectacular palate (and those of her daughter, Lily, and husband, Doug Tidwell), and gave me essential feedback.

My deepest thanks to Katie Brucker (and fiancé Nick, too!) for being the first-out-of-the-gate tester, for compiling facts, and mostly for being the best cheerleader I could ask for.

And as always, a huge thank-you to photographer Maren Caruso, stylist Robyn Valarik, and prop stylist Ethel Brennan for creating a week of fun and photographic beauty.

To the cheesemakers—where would I be without you? And where would this book be without the cheeses you so generously gave me to work with in the service of recipe development? My heartfelt thanks to Wendy Mitchell of Avalanche Dairy (Todd and Kevin, too!); Allison Hooper of Vermont Butter & Cheese Creamery; Francis Plowman, David Gremmels, and Cary Bryant of Rogue Creamery; Tara Kirch and Steve Margaritas of Best Cheese and Coach Farm; the Giacomini family of Pt. Reyes Farmstead Cheese Company; Bob McCall, Janne Rasmussen, and Mary Keehn of Cypress Grove; and Mike Matucheski, Chad Vincent, and Jim Sartori of Sartori Cheese.

Then there are the tasters, whose enthusiasm about what they were tasting was just as valuable as their crucial input. First and foremost, to the staff and volunteers at the UCSF Cancer Resource Center in San Francisco. They took their roles as tasters as seriously as they do their own good work and made this book better in the process. To my cousin, Miles Keilin, for nibbling on my recipe experiments, never revealing that he hates mac & cheese, and to his mom, Kim, for being a loyal mac & cheese fan and friend; to Faye Keogh, Kevin Donahue, and Beth Roemer, whose effusiveness peppered with laughter made for great memories as well as helpful input; to dear friends Linda and Kelly Hayes, whose formidable culinary skills and sophisticated palates made their feedback ever more valuable; ditto for Pam Weber and Richard Rosenfeld, Delicious Karma's Michelle and Jim Ritchie, and the unparalleled Joyce Goldstein, whose culinary advice—and friendship—is priceless. Thanks to Ellen Walbert for contributing her recipe for arguably the best noodle kugel ever, and to Joan and Alan Hayman, who generously and convincingly weighed in on the cover design to ensure it would be what you see now.

Finally, and always, my family. To my sister, Andi, who enthusiastically rounded up her colleagues at the UCSF Cancer Resource Center to taste and commit their comments to paper, and then delivered the results proudly, including her own invaluable comments; to Val, who dutifully did the same; to my mom who, as always, provided her quiet support and overt enthusiasm about yet another cheese book; and to Dad, who didn't make it to see the final product but who nevertheless edited it right alongside me.

appendix

MAC & CHEESE RESTAURANTS

west
Homeroom
Oakland, California
www.homeroom510.com
Elbows Mac n' Cheese
Cerritos, California
www.elbowsmacandcheese.com
Paddy Mac
Los Angeles, California
www.eatpaddymac.com
Herb's Mac & Cheese
Portland, Oregon
www.herbsmacandcheese.com
Mac! Mac & Cheesery
Portland, Oregon
www.macandcheese.biz
MacShack
Las Vegas, Nevada
www.macaronishack.com

south
Jus' Mac
Houston, Texas
www.jusmac.com
Jus' Mac
Sugar Land, Texas
www.jusmac.com
Macnfoodtruck (Vegan)
Miami, Florida
www.macnfoodtruck.com

midwest
The Southern Mac & Cheese Truck
Chicago, Illinois
www.thesouthernmac.com
The Southern Mac & Cheese Store
60 E. Lake St, Chicago, Illinois
www.thesouthernmac.com
Cheese-ology
University City, Missouri
www.cheese-ology.com

northeast
Macdaddy's
Monroe, Connecticut
www.macdaddyrestaurants.com
MMMac & Cheese
Boston, Massachusetts
http://www.mmmacncheese.com/

various locations
Mr. Macs
Manchester, New Hampshire
www.mr-macs.com
S'Mac
New York City
www.smacnyc.com
MacBar
New York City
www.macbar.net

nationwide
Noodles & Company
www.noodles.com

Metric Conversions and Equivalents

Metric Conversion Formulas

TO CONVERT	MULTIPLY
Ounces to grams	Ounces by 28.35
Pounds to kilograms	Pounds by .454
Teaspoons to milliliters	Teaspoons by 4.93
Tablespoons to milliliters	Tablespoons by 14.79
Fluid ounces to milliliters	Fluid ounces by 29.57
Cups to milliliters	Cups by 236.59
Cups to liters	Cups by .236
Pints to liters	Pints by .473
Quarts to liters	Quarts by .946
Gallons to liters	Gallons by 3.785
Inches to centimeters	Inches by 2.54

Approximate Metric Equivalents

VOLUME	
¼ teaspoon	1 milliliter
½ teaspoon	2.5 milliliters
¾ teaspoon	4 milliliters
1 teaspoon	5 milliliters
1¼ teaspoons	6 milliliters
1½ teaspoons	7.5 milliliters
1¾ teaspoons	8.5 milliliters
2 teaspoons	10 milliliters
1 tablespoon (½ fluid ounce)	15 milliliters
2 tablespoons (1 fluid ounce)	30 milliliters
¼ cup	60 milliliters
⅓ cup	80 milliliters
½ cup (4 fluid ounces)	120 milliliters
⅔ cup	160 milliliters
¾ cup	180 milliliters
1 cup (8 fluid ounces)	240 milliliters
1¼ cups	300 milliliters
1½ cups (12 fluid ounces)	360 milliliters
1⅔ cups	400 milliliters
2 cups (1 pint)	460 milliliters
3 cups	700 milliliters
4 cups (1 quart)	.95 liter
1 quart plus ¼ cup	1 liter
4 quarts (1 gallon)	3.8 liters

WEIGHT

¼ ounce	7 grams
½ ounce	14 grams
¾ ounce	21 grams
1 ounce	28 grams
1¼ ounces	35 grams
1½ ounces	42.5 grams
1⅔ ounces	45 grams
2 ounces	57 grams
3 ounces	85 grams
4 ounces (¼ pound)	113 grams
5 ounces	142 grams
6 ounces	170 grams
7 ounces	198 grams
8 ounces (½ pound)	227 grams
16 ounces (1 pound)	454 grams
35.25 ounces (2.2 pounds)	1 kilogram

LENGTH

⅛ inch	3 millimeters
¼ inch	6 millimeters
½ inch	1¼ centimeters
1 inch	2½ centimeters
2 inches	5 centimeters
2½ inches	6 centimeters
4 inches	10 centimeters
5 inches	13 centimeters
6 inches	15¼ centimeters
12 inches (1 foot)	30 centimeters

Information compiled from a variety of sources, including *Recipes into Type* by Joan Whitman and Dolores Simon (Newton, MA: Biscuit Books, 2000); *The New Food Lover's Companion* by Sharon Tyler Herbst (Hauppauge, NY: Barron's, 1995); and *Rosemary Brown's Big Kitchen Instruction Book* (Kansas City, MO: Andrews McMeel, 1998).

mac & cheese, please!

index

a

Accarino, Matthew, 104
Andouille, Colby, and Mustard
Mac & Cheese, 76–77
Appenzeller, xvii
Asiago, xvii, xix
Herbed Zucchini, Havarti, and
Whole-Grain Mac & Cheese,
133–34

b

bacon, 4, 9, 60, 96, 131. See also
Canadian bacon; pancetta
Cheddar, Bacon, Roasted
Tomato, and Tabasco Mac &
Cheese, 16–19
Gruyère, Caramelized Onion,
Blue Cheese, and Bacon
Mac & Cheese, 82–84
Mushroom, Bacon, and Eggs
Mac & Cheese, 91–92
baking dishes, xxvi–xxvii
beef, ground, 50, 84
Mediterranean Mac & Cheese,
117–18
Bel Paese, xvii
bell peppers. See peppers
blue cheese, xx
Buffalo Chicken and Crispy
Skin Mac & Cheese, 144–47
French Cheese and Savoy
Cabbage Mac & Cheese,
30–32
Fruit and (Mac &) Cheese,
101–2
Gruyère, Caramelized Onion,
Blue Cheese, and Bacon
Mac & Cheese, 82–84
"Paella" Mac & Cheese, 148–49
Smokey Blue with Leeks and
Hazelnuts Mac & Cheese,
35–37

bread crumbs, xiv
making, xxiii–xxiv
breakfast for dinner, 81–102
"Eggs Benedict" Mac & Cheese,
85–87
Fruit and (Mac &) Cheese,
101–2
Gruyère, Caramelized Onion,
Blue Cheese, and Bacon
Mac & Cheese, 82–84
Huevos Rancheros Mac &
Cheese, 97–100
Mushroom, Bacon, and Eggs
Mac & Cheese, 91–92
Spicy "Home Fries" Mac &
Cheese, 93–96
Waffle Mac & Cheese, 88–89
Brie, xii, xx
French Cheese and Savoy
Cabbage Mac & Cheese,
30–32
Truffle, Cream, and Mushroom
Mac & Cheese, 42–43
Broccoli, Cheddar, and Crispy
Shallot Mac & Cheese, 57–60
Buffalo Chicken and Crispy Skin
Mac & Cheese, 144–47
Fried Mac & Cheese Squares,
21–22
burrata, xvii
Sauce-and-Meatballs Mac &
Cheese with Burrata, 73–75
butter, xiv
Butternut Squash, Gruyère, and
Brown Butter Mac & Cheese,
113–14

c

Camembert, xx
Canadian bacon: "Eggs Benedict"
Mac & Cheese, 85–87
cashews, 54
Chalet Cheese Cooperative, 10

cheddar, xvii
Broccoli, Cheddar, and Crispy
Shallot Mac & Cheese,
57–60
Buffalo Chicken and Crispy
Skin Mac & Cheese, 144–47
Cheddar, Bacon, Roasted
Tomato, and Tabasco Mac &
Cheese, 16–19
Cheddar, Ham, Apple, and
Spiced Pecan Mac & Cheese,
62–64
Classic Mac & Cheese, 3–4
Gluten-Free Classic Mac &
Cheese, 7–9
Huevos Rancheros Mac &
Cheese, 97–100
Light(er) Cheddar and Arugula
Mac & Cheese with
Croutons, 130–31
Mac & Cheese Meets Grilled
Cheese, 27–29
Nacho Mac & Cheese, 150–53
Spicy "Home Fries" Mac &
Cheese, 93–96
stovetop Classic Mac &
Cheese, 5–6
Vermont Cheddar Mac &
Cheese with Ham and
Maple-Pickled Onions,
70–71
cheese, xii–xiii. See also sauce;
specific types
grating, xiii, xvi
types, xvi–xx
Cheshire, xvii
chèvre. See goat cheese
chicken, 60, 129, 153
Buffalo Chicken and Crispy
Skin Mac & Cheese, 144–47
Chicken, Pesto, and Provolone
Mac & Cheese, 107–9

chiles. *See also* hot sauce
Fiery South of the Border Mac & Cheese, 127–29
chorizo, Spanish, 25
"Paella" Mac & Cheese, 148–49
Ciabatta Croutons, Pizza Mac & Cheese with, 139–41
classic mac & cheese, 1–22
Cheddar, Bacon, Roasted Tomato, and Tabasco Mac & Cheese, 16–19
Classic Mac & Cheese, 3–4
Classic Mac & Cheese (stovetop version), 5–6
Fried Mac & Cheese Squares, 21–22
Gluten-Free Classic Mac & Cheese, 7–9
Kevin's Mac & Cheese (Velveeta, Baby!), 14–15
Wisconsin Cheese, Brats, and Onion Mac & Cheese, 10–13
Coach Farm Grating Stick, xix
Colby, xvii
Andouille, Colby, and Mustard Mac & Cheese, 76–77
Wisconsin Cheese, Brats, and Onion Mac & Cheese, 10–13
Colby-Jack, xvii, 76
Comté, xvii
French Cheese and Savoy Cabbage Mac & Cheese, 30–32
Crab, Artichoke, and Swiss Mac & Cheese, 119–20
cream, xiii, xxiv–xxv
Truffle, Cream, and Mushroom Mac & Cheese, 42–43
cream cheese
Buffalo Chicken and Crispy Skin Mac & Cheese, 144–47
Ellen's Noodle Kugel, 142–43
Mad Men Mac & Cheese, 136–37
Crescenza, xvii
Pizza Mac & Cheese with Ciabatta Croutons, 139–41

d

decadent mac & cheese, 103–20
Butternut Squash, Gruyère, and Brown Butter Mac & Cheese, 113–14
Chicken, Pesto, and Provolone Mac & Cheese, 107–9
Crab, Artichoke, and Swiss Mac & Cheese, 119–20
Mediterranean Mac & Cheese, 117–18
Parmesan, Pea, Prosciutto, and Basil Mac & Cheese, 110–11
Smoky Silky Parsnip, Mushroom, and Espresso Mac & Cheese, 104–5
Truffle Mac & Cheese, 115–16
Donahue, Kevin, 14
dry Jack, xix
Sonoma Mac & Cheese, 33–34
Dubliner, xvii

e

Eggplant Parmesan Mac & Cheese, 47–50
eggs, 16, 19
"Eggs Benedict" Mac & Cheese, 85–87
Ellen's Noodle Kugel, 142–43
Huevos Rancheros Mac & Cheese, 97–100
Mushroom, Bacon, and Eggs Mac & Cheese, 91–92
Ellen's Noodle Kugel, 142–43
Emmentaler, xvii
Epoisses, xx
Espresso BellaVitano: Smoky Silky Parsnip, Mushroom, and Espresso Mac & Cheese, 104–5
Explorateur, xx
Truffle, Cream, and Mushroom Mac & Cheese, 42–43

f

feta, xx
Mediterranean Mac & Cheese, 117–18

Fiery South of the Border Mac & Cheese, 127–29
Flagship, xvii
Fontina, xvii, xix
"Eggs Benedict" Mac & Cheese, 85–87
Garlicky Italian Mac & Cheese, 39–40
Mac & Cheese Meets Grilled Cheese, 27–29
Truffle Mac & Cheese, 115–16
Zesty Kale Two Ways and Fontina Mac & Cheese, 45–46
French Cheese and Savoy Cabbage Mac & Cheese, 30–32
fresh goat cheese. *See* goat cheese
Fried Mac & Cheese Squares, 21–22
fried shallots, 54
Broccoli, Cheddar, and Crispy Shallot Mac & Cheese, 57–60
fromage blanc, xx
Fromager d'Affinois, xix
Fruit and (Mac &) Cheese, 101–2

g

Gloucester, xix
gluten-free mac & cheese, xxvi
Gluten-Free Classic Mac & Cheese, 7–9
goat cheese, xii–xiii, xx, 131. *See also specific types*
Goat Cheese, Mozzarella, Basil, and Tomato Mac & Cheese, 124–25
"Paella" Mac & Cheese, 148–49
Sonoma Mac & Cheese, 33–34
Spring Vegetable and Whole-Grain Mac & Cheese, 55–56
Waffle Mac & Cheese, 88–89
Gorgonzola. *See also* blue cheese
Fruit and (Mac &) Cheese, 101–2
"Paella" Mac & Cheese, 148–49

Gouda, xvii, xix
    Buffalo Chicken and Crispy
        Skin Mac & Cheese, 144–47
Grana Padano, xix
grilled cheese sandwiches: Mac &
    Cheese Meets Grilled Cheese,
    27–29
Gruyère, xvii, xix
    Butternut Squash, Gruyère, and
        Brown Butter Mac & Cheese,
        113–14
    Classic Mac & Cheese, 3–4
    Crab, Artichoke, and Swiss Mac
        & Cheese, 119–20
    Gluten-Free Classic Mac &
        Cheese, 7–9
    Gruyère, Caramelized Onion,
        Blue Cheese, and Bacon
        Mac & Cheese, 82–84
    Mushroom, Bacon, and Eggs
        Mac & Cheese, 91–92
    Parmesan, Pea, Prosciutto, and
        Basil Mac & Cheese, 110–11
    Spring Vegetable and Whole-
        Grain Mac & Cheese, 55–56
    stovetop Classic Mac &
        Cheese, 5–6
guacamole, 153
    Nacho Mac & Cheese, 150–53

h

Halloumi, xx
ham, 25, 32, 56, 137. *See also*
    prosciutto
    Cheddar, Ham, Apple, and
        Spiced Pecan Mac & Cheese,
        62–64
    Vermont Cheddar Mac &
        Cheese with Ham and
        Maple-Pickled Onions,
        70–71
Havarti, xvii
    Herbed Zucchini, Havarti, and
        Whole-Grain Mac & Cheese,
        133–34

Indian-Spiced Roasted
    Cauliflower and Spinach
    Mac & Cheese, 51–54
Prosciutto and Pine Nut
    Mac & Cheese, 79–80
Hayes, Kelly, 73
Hayes, Linda, 73
Herbed Zucchini, Havarti, and
    Whole-Grain Mac & Cheese,
    133–34
"Home Fries" Mac & Cheese,
    Spicy, 93–96
hot sauce, 6
    Buffalo Chicken and Crispy
        Skin Mac & Cheese, 144–47
    Cheddar, Bacon, Roasted
        Tomato, and Tabasco Mac &
        Cheese, 16–19
    Fried Mac & Cheese Squares,
        21–22
    Spicy "Home Fries" Mac &
        Cheese, 93–96
    Spicy Reuben Mac & Cheese,
        68–69
Huevos Rancheros Mac & Cheese,
    97–100

i

Indian-Spiced Roasted
    Cauliflower and Spinach Mac
    & Cheese, 51–54
individual servings, xxvi–xxvii
Italian Mac & Cheese, Garlicky,
    39–40

j

jam, tomato, 54
Jarlsberg, xvii
    Asparagus, Swiss, and Dill Mac
        & Cheese, 122–23
    Crab, Artichoke, and Swiss Mac
        & Cheese, 119–20
Jefferson, Thomas, xi

k

Kevin's Mac & Cheese (Velveeta,
    Baby!), 14–15

l

La Tur, xx
lamb, ground, 50
    Mediterranean Mac & Cheese,
        117–18
leftovers, xxvii–xxviii
light mac & cheese, viii, xxv,
    121–34
    Asparagus, Swiss, and Dill Mac
        & Cheese, 122–23
    Fiery South of the Border Mac
        & Cheese, 127–29
    Goat Cheese, Mozzarella, Basil,
        and Tomato Mac & Cheese,
        124–25
    Herbed Zucchini, Havarti, and
        Whole-Grain Mac & Cheese,
        133–34
    Light(er) Cheddar and Arugula
        Mac & Cheese with
        Croutons, 130–31
Limburger, 10
    Wisconsin Cheese, Brats, and
        Onion Mac & Cheese, 10–13
lower-fat recipes. *See* light mac
    & cheese

m

macaroni. *See* pasta
Mad Men Mac & Cheese, 136–37
Mahón, xix
manchego, xix
    Mediterranean Mac & Cheese,
        117–18
    "Paella" Mac & Cheese, 148–49
    Spanish Mac & Cheese, 24–25
mascarpone, xx
    Fruit and (Mac &) Cheese,
        101–2
    Mac & Cheese Meets Grilled
        Cheese, 27–29
measurements, xv, 157–58
Mediterranean Mac & Cheese,
    117–18
metric equivalents, 157–58

Mexican flavors
Fiery South of the Border Mac & Cheese, 127–29
Huevos Rancheros Mac & Cheese, 97–100
Nacho Mac & Cheese, 150–53
Midnight Moon, xix
milk, xiii, xxiv–xxv
Mimolette, xix
Monterey Jack, xvii. See also dry Jack; pepper Jack
Andouille, Colby, and Mustard Mac & Cheese, 76–77
Huevos Rancheros Mac & Cheese, 97–100
mozzarella, xvii. See also smoked mozzarella
Eggplant Parmesan Mac & Cheese, 47–50
Garlicky Italian Mac & Cheese, 39–40
Goat Cheese, Mozzarella, Basil, and Tomato Mac & Cheese, 124–25
Pizza Mac & Cheese with Ciabatta Croutons, 139–41
Salami, Fennel, Pepper, and Mozzarella mac & cheese, 65–66
Sauce-and-Meatballs Mac & Cheese with Burrata, 73–75
Smokey Blue with Leeks and Hazelnuts Mac & Cheese, 35–37
Mt. Tam, xx
Sonoma Mac & Cheese, 33–34
Muenster, xvii
muffin-size portions, xxvi–xxvii

n

Nacho Mac & Cheese, 150–53
Noodle Kugel, Ellen's, 142–43
nuts. See specific types

o

Olson, Myron, 10
Ossau-Iraty, xix

oven-roasted tomatoes, 4, 9, 16–17, 29, 131
Herbed Zucchini, Havarti, and Whole-Grain Mac & Cheese, 133–34
Pizza Mac & Cheese with Ciabatta Croutons, 139–41

p

"Paella" Mac & Cheese, 148–49
pancetta, 29, 114, 147
paneer, xx
Indian-Spiced Roasted Cauliflower and Spinach Mac & Cheese, 51–54
Parmesan. See also Parmigiano-Reggiano
Butternut Squash, Gruyère, and Brown Butter Mac & Cheese, 113–14
Goat Cheese, Mozzarella, Basil, and Tomato Mac & Cheese, 124–25
Salami, Fennel, Pepper, and Mozzarella mac & cheese, 65–66
Truffle Mac & Cheese, 115–16
Parmigiano-Reggiano, xii, xix
Classic Mac & Cheese, 3–4
Crab, Artichoke, and Swiss Mac & Cheese, 119–20
Eggplant Parmesan Mac & Cheese, 47–50
Garlicky Italian Mac & Cheese, 39–40
Gluten-Free Classic Mac & Cheese, 7–9
Parmesan, Pea, Prosciutto, and Basil Mac & Cheese, 110–11
Prosciutto and Pine Nut Mac & Cheese, 79–80
stovetop Classic Mac & Cheese, 5–6
Parrano, xix
party time mac & cheese, xv, 135–53
Buffalo Chicken and Crispy Skin Mac & Cheese, 144–47

Ellen's Noodle Kugel, 142–43
Mad Men Mac & Cheese, 136–37
Nacho Mac & Cheese, 150–53
"Paella" Mac & Cheese, 148–49
Pizza Mac & Cheese with Ciabatta Croutons, 139–41
pasta
cooking, xiii–xiv
gluten-free, xxvi, 7
types, xxii–xxiii
pastrami: Spicy Reuben Mac & Cheese, 68–69
pecorino, xix. See also Pecorino Romano
Pizza Mac & Cheese with Ciabatta Croutons, 139–41
Pecorino Romano
Butternut Squash, Gruyère, and Brown Butter Mac & Cheese, 113–14
Classic Mac & Cheese, 3–4
Crab, Artichoke, and Swiss Mac & Cheese, 119–20
Eggplant Parmesan Mac & Cheese, 47–50
Garlicky Italian Mac & Cheese, 39–40
Gluten-Free Classic Mac & Cheese, 7–9
Prosciutto and Pine Nut Mac & Cheese, 79–80
Salami, Fennel, Pepper, and Mozzarella mac & cheese, 65–66
stovetop Classic Mac & Cheese, 5–6
Truffle Mac & Cheese, 115–16
Zesty Kale Two Ways and Fontina Mac & Cheese, 45–46
pepper Jack
Fiery South of the Border Mac & Cheese, 127–29
Nacho Mac & Cheese, 150–53
peppers, 4, 9, 141
Mediterranean Mac & Cheese, 117–18

Salami, Fennel, Pepper, and Mozzarella mac & cheese, 65–66

Spanish Mac & Cheese, 24–25

Spicy "Home Fries" Mac & Cheese, 93–96

Petit Basque, xix
Mediterranean Mac & Cheese, 117–18

Piave vecchio, xix

piquillo peppers: Spanish Mac & Cheese, 24–25

Pizza Mac & Cheese with Ciabatta Croutons, 139–41

Pleasant Ridge Reserve, xix

Point Reyes Toma, xix
Sonoma Mac & Cheese, 33–34

pork, ground: Sauce-and-Meatballs Mac & Cheese with Burrata, 73–75

Port-Salut, xvii

portions, xv–xvi, xxvi–xxvii

potato chips, as add-in, 137

prosciutto, 40
Parmesan, Pea, Prosciutto, and Basil Mac & Cheese, 110–11

Prosciutto and Pine Nut Mac & Cheese, 79–80

protein mac & cheese, 61–80
Andouille, Colby, and Mustard Mac & Cheese, 76–77

Cheddar, Ham, Apple, and Spiced Pecan Mac & Cheese, 62–64

Prosciutto and Pine Nut Mac & Cheese, 79–80

Salami, Fennel, Pepper, and Mozzarella mac & cheese, 65–66

Sauce-and-Meatballs Mac & Cheese with Burrata, 73–75

Spicy Reuben Mac & Cheese, 68–69

Vermont Cheddar Mac & Cheese with Ham and Maple-Pickled Onions, 70–71

provolone, xvii
Chicken, Pesto, and Provolone Mac & Cheese, 107–9

q

queso blanco, xx

queso fresco: Nacho Mac & Cheese, 150–53

r

Raclette, xix

Randolph, Mary, xi

red peppers. *See* peppers

reduced-fat cheese, xxv, 133. *See also* light mac & cheese

reheating, xxvii–xxviii

restaurants, 156

ricotta, xx
Asparagus, Swiss, and Dill Mac & Cheese, 122–23

Waffle Mac & Cheese, 88–89

ricotta salata, xix
Mediterranean Mac & Cheese, 117–18

roasted garlic, 141

roasted peppers. *See* peppers

roasted tomatoes. *See* oven-roasted tomatoes

Robiola, xx

Rogue Creamery, 35

Roquefort. *See also* blue cheese
French Cheese and Savoy Cabbage Mac & Cheese, 30–32

s

Saint-André, xx
Truffle, Cream, and Mushroom Mac & Cheese, 42–43

Saint Marcellin, xx

salami, 6
Salami, Fennel, Pepper, and Mozzarella mac & cheese, 65–66

salsa
Fiery South of the Border Mac & Cheese, 127–29

Huevos Rancheros Mac & Cheese, 97–100

Nacho Mac & Cheese, 150–53

salt
in pasta water, xiii–xiv
salted butter, xiv

sandwiches: Mac & Cheese Meets Grilled Cheese, 27–29

SarVecchio, xix

sauce, xiv, xxv–xxvi
gluten-free, 7
quick, xxv–xxvi

Sauce-and-Meatballs Mac & Cheese with Burrata, 73–75

sausage, 96
Andouille, Colby, and Mustard Mac & Cheese, 76–77

Wisconsin Cheese, Brats, and Onion Mac & Cheese, 10–13

Serrano ham, as add-in, 25

serving sizes, xv–xvi, xxvi–xxvii

shallots, fried, 54
Broccoli, Cheddar, and Crispy Shallot Mac & Cheese, 57–60

shrimp: "Paella" Mac & Cheese, 148–49

smoked mozzarella
Smokey Blue with Leeks and Hazelnuts Mac & Cheese, 35–37

Smoky Silky Parsnip, Mushroom, and Espresso Mac & Cheese, 104–5

Spicy Reuben Mac & Cheese, 68–69

Smokey Blue with Leeks and Hazelnuts Mac & Cheese, 35–37

Smoky Silky Parsnip, Mushroom, and Espresso Mac & Cheese, 104–5

Spicy Reuben Mac & Cheese, 68–69

Sonoma Mac & Cheese, 33–34

Spanish Mac & Cheese, 24–25

Spicy "Home Fries" Mac & Cheese, 93–96

Spicy Reuben Mac & Cheese, 68–69

SPQR, 104

Spring Vegetable and Whole-Grain Mac & Cheese, 55–56

stovetop mac & cheese, xvi, xviii, xxvii
advance preparation, xv
Andouille, Colby, and Mustard Mac & Cheese, 76–77
Asparagus, Swiss, and Dill Mac & Cheese, 122–23
Classic Mac & Cheese, 5–6
Fiery South of the Border Mac & Cheese, 127–29
Fruit and (Mac &) Cheese, 101–2
Goat Cheese, Mozzarella, Basil, and Tomato Mac & Cheese, 124–25
Herbed Zucchini, Havarti, and Whole-Grain Mac & Cheese, 133–34
Indian-Spiced Roasted Cauliflower and Spinach Mac & Cheese, 51–54
Light(er) Cheddar and Arugula Mac & Cheese with Croutons, 130–31
Mac & Cheese Meets Grilled Cheese, 27–29
Mediterranean Mac & Cheese, 117–18
"Paella" Mac & Cheese, 148–49
Parmesan, Pea, Prosciutto, and Basil Mac & Cheese, 110–11
reheating, xxviii
Salami, Fennel, Pepper, and Mozzarella mac & cheese, 65–66
Spanish Mac & Cheese, 24–25
Spicy Reuben Mac & Cheese, 68–69
Spring Vegetable and Whole-Grain Mac & Cheese, 55–56
Truffle, Cream, and Mushroom Mac & Cheese, 42–43
sweet mac & cheese: Ellen's Noodle Kugel, 142–43

Swiss, xvii
Asparagus, Swiss, and Dill Mac & Cheese, 122–23
Crab, Artichoke, and Swiss Mac & Cheese, 119–20

t
Taleggio, xx
Garlicky Italian Mac & Cheese, 39–40
Prosciutto and Pine Nut Mac & Cheese, 79–80
Sauce-and-Meatballs Mac & Cheese with Burrata, 73–75
tomato sauce, chunky, 47
Eggplant Parmesan Mac & Cheese, 47–50
Sauce-and-Meatballs Mac & Cheese with Burrata, 73–75
tomatoes, 4, 9, 29, 40, 60, 131
Cheddar, Bacon, Roasted Tomato, and Tabasco Mac & Cheese, 16–19
Goat Cheese, Mozzarella, Basil, and Tomato Mac & Cheese, 124–25
Herbed Zucchini, Havarti, and Whole-Grain Mac & Cheese, 133–34
Indian-Spiced Roasted Cauliflower and Spinach Mac & Cheese, 51–54
oven-roasted, 16–17
Pizza Mac & Cheese with Ciabatta Croutons, 139–41
Prosciutto and Pine Nut Mac & Cheese, 79–80
tomato jam, 54
truffles
Truffle, Cream, and Mushroom Mac & Cheese, 42–43
Truffle Mac & Cheese, 115–16

v
vegetable mac & cheese, 41–60
Broccoli, Cheddar, and Crispy Shallot Mac & Cheese, 57–60
Eggplant Parmesan Mac & Cheese, 47–50
Indian-Spiced Roasted Cauliflower and Spinach Mac & Cheese, 51–54
Spring Vegetable and Whole-Grain Mac & Cheese, 55–56
Truffle, Cream, and Mushroom Mac & Cheese, 42–43
Zesty Kale Two Ways and Fontina Mac & Cheese, 45–46
Velveeta, xvii
Kevin's Mac & Cheese (Velveeta, Baby!), 14–15
Mad Men Mac & Cheese, 136–37
Vermont Cheddar Mac & Cheese with Ham and Maple-Pickled Onions, 70–71
The Virginia Cookbook (Randolph), xi

w
Waffle Mac & Cheese, 88–89
Wensleydale, xix
whole-grain pasta
Herbed Zucchini, Havarti, and Whole-Grain Mac & Cheese, 133–34
Spring Vegetable and Whole-Grain Mac & Cheese, 55–56
Wisconsin Cheese, Brats, and Onion Mac & Cheese, 10–13

z
Zesty Kale Two Ways and Fontina Mac & Cheese, 45–46